TEACHING COLLOCATION

Further developments in the Lexical Approach

Editor: Michael Lewis

with chapters by

Jane Conzett
Peter Hargreaves
Jimmie Hill
Michael Hoey
Michael Lewis
Morgan Lewis
George Woolard

HEINLE
CENGAGE Learning

Australia • Brazil • Japan • Korea • Mexico • Singapore • Spain • United Kingdom • United States

HEINLE
CENGAGE Learning™

Teaching Collocation:
Further Developments in the
Lexical Approach
Michael Lewis

Editorial Director / Global ELT: Joe
Dougherty

Executive Marketing Manager / Global
ELT/ESL: Amy Mabley

Cover Design: Anna Macleod

Acknowledgements

Firstly, I must thank the authors of the
individual chapters for their contributions and their co-operation. I am also
particularly grateful to Jimmie Hill,
Morgan Lewis and Clare West, who
provided valuable insights on the overall
shape and detailed contents of the
book.

Many teachers have discussed the ideas
contained in this book, in correspon-
dence, by e-mail, in publised articles
and face-to-face at conferences. Many
suggestions in this book are based on
these discussions. I acknowledge all of
these colleagues with gratitude, but
particularly Maggie Baigent, Deborah
Petty, John Sinclair, Graham Smith, Peter
Sunderland, Svetlana Ter-Minasova,
Scott Thornbury, and Annie Williams, all
of whose ideas are explicitly mentioned.
Special thanks to Jon Wright, who drew
my attention to the remarkable O.
Henry story which makes up Chapter 6.

We are grateful to the following for
permission to reproduce copyright
material:

Oxford Univeristy Press for a short
extract from *New Headway Intermediate*.

Cambridge University Press for a short
extract from *English Vocabulary in Use*.

For permission to use material from this text
or product, submit all requests online at
cengage.com/permissions
Further permissions questions can be emailed to
permissionrequest@cengage.com

ISBN: 978-1-899396-11-5

Heinle
High Holborn House, 50-51 Bedford Row
London WC1R 4LR

Cengage Learning is a leading provider of
customised learning solutions with office
locations around the globe, including
Singapore, the United Kingdom, Australia,
Mexico, Brazil and Japan. Locate our local
office at: **international.cengage.com/region**

Cengage Learning products are represented in
Canada by Nelson Education, Ltd.

Visit Heinle online at **http://elt.heinle.com**
Visit our corporate website at
www.**cengage.com**

The contributors

Jane Conzett has taught ESL for many years. She runs the Intensive English Program at Xavier University, Cincinnati, Ohio.

Peter Hargreaves is Head of the English as a Foreign Language section of the University of Cambridge Local Examinations Syndicate (UCLES).

Jimmie Hill taught English in Sweden and the UK. He has given teacher training lectures and seminars in many countries, written many articles and is the co-author of *The Working Week,* and *Grammar and Practice.* He is co-founder and Editorial Director of LTP.

Michael Hoey is Professor of English Language and Director of the Applied English Language Studies Unit at the University of Liverpool. He has published many papers and books on descriptive linguistics and is author of the award-winning *Patterns of Lexis in Text.*

Michael Lewis is co-founder of LTP. He has written many articles and books, including *Practical Techniques for Language Teaching, The Lexical Approach* and *Implementing the Lexical Approach.*

Morgan Lewis has taught EFL for over ten years. He has extensive teacher training experience in Britain and abroad. He has recently co-authored and edited lexically-based EFL materials.

George Woolard is an experienced ELT teacher who has worked in Greece and Malaysia. He currently teaches a wide range of courses at Stevenson College, Edinburgh.

Contents

Introduction

As David Wilkins observed many years ago, 'Without grammar little can be conveyed; without vocabulary nothing can be conveyed.' The single most important task facing language learners is acquiring a sufficiently large vocabulary. We now recognise that much of our 'vocabulary' consists of prefabricated chunks of different kinds. The single most important kind of chunk is collocation. Self-evidently, then, teaching collocation should be a top priority in every language course.

The centrality of lexis

Increasingly, language teachers have turned to the question of how language is stored in the brain. If native speakers store large amounts of language in chunks, what strategies should language teachers adopt if they are to help learners build mental lexicons which are similarly phrasal?

From a teaching point of view, arguments about exactly what types of multi-word item make up the mental lexicon are unfruitful. It is clear that the learners' task in acquiring a sufficiently large mental lexicon is considerably greater than we previously thought. Although grammar remains an important part of language acquisition, the lexical memory load, even for an intermediate learner, is enormous. We now recognise that the principal difference between intermediate and advanced learners is not complex grammar, but the greatly expanded mental lexicon available to advanced learners. Failure by some teachers to recognise this simple fact can condemn their learners to a lifetime on the intermediate plateau.

A modified role for grammar

The centrality of lexis means that the teaching of traditional grammar structures should play a less important role than in the past. Recognising that every word has its own grammar, however, means that any approach based on the central role of lexis is in many ways more grammatical than any traditional grammar syllabus.

Three themes

Three themes re-occur regularly in this book:
- The mental lexicon is larger than we previously thought.
- The prefabricated chunks stored in our mental lexicons ready for use are often larger than previously recognised.
- Really 'knowing a word' involves knowing its grammar – the patterns in which it is regularly used.

The contributors all argue that expanding learners' phrasal lexicons and knowledge of word grammar are the two most important elements of any language course. There is a serious challenge for teachers if our new insights into the size, importance and nature of the mental lexicon are not simply to overwhelm students. Mike McCarthy once eloquently described the 'vocabulary' part of language learning as mastering 'the chaos of the lexicon'. Everything in this book is designed to help bring order to that chaos for both teachers and, more importantly, their learners.

Developing the Lexical Approach

The Lexical Approach (1993) was a combination of applied linguistics and language teaching methodology. *Implementing the Lexical Approach* (1997) was, as its title suggests, more practical; methodology, rather than applied linguistics. The first half of this book is even more practical. The chapters arise not from what teachers **could** do in their classrooms, but from what they are already doing. Some of the suggestions are modest; others are more radical, involving a reversal of traditional priorities. Introducing modest changes, in a climate of action research, is surely the best way forward.

Increasing understanding

Several contributors stress their own increasing understanding of collocation. The basic idea is extremely simple – some words co-occur in interesting ways. But a great deal lies behind that formulation. Frequent collocation *(nice day)*, is quite different from strong collocation *(wage war)*; but neither the most frequent nor the strongest are the most useful for learners. Only teachers who have a clear understanding of different kinds of collocation will be able to help learners in the best possible way. Part 2 of this book is designed to help teachers develop this clearer understanding.

From practice to theory

Books of this kind tend to go from theory to practice; this book reverses that order. The authors in Part 1 describe how what they do in class has changed as a result of their developing awareness of the lexical nature of language. Part 2 describes in more detail the present state of our understanding of language and acquisition. Teachers who have tried some of the suggestions in Part 1, and want to take their understanding further, should turn particularly to Chapters 7 and 8. Teachers with a lot of experience of lexically-based teaching, or those on in-service courses may prefer to read these two chapters first, before returning to the more detailed practical suggestions of Part 1.

The contributors to this book have one principal objective – to develop learners' mental lexicons, and with that, to give those learners a far wider range of life-choices. It is a worthwhile objective.

Michael Lewis, Hove, January 2000

Chapter 1

There is nothing as practical as a good theory

Morgan Lewis

Morgan Lewis describes how his initial teacher training led him to value grammar and explaining, and to believe both in the importance of a good lesson plan and the close relationship between what he taught and what his students learned. Experience led him to question these ideas and, as a result of more theoretical study of the nature of both language and learning, to change his classroom priorities. A better understanding of language means he gives much more attention to collocation in all his classes; a better understanding of language acquisition means consciously bringing more language into every class, while accepting that the teacher cannot be sure exactly what learners will do with the language which is presented to them. He believes many teachers with a few years experience behind them will recognise the story he tells.

1.1 Introduction

Seeing the title of this chapter, you might have assumed that the chapter was written by an applied linguist who will remove you from the classroom into the far off land of academia. In fact, I am a regular classroom teacher with about ten years' experience of teaching mostly multi-lingual classes in the UK.

Perhaps like you, after a few years in the classroom, I began to question some of the received wisdom of my initial training. The Present–Practise–Produce paradigm I started with seemed such a neat, tidy and sensible way to go about teaching. I increasingly found, however, that learning did not follow the same tidy model. I seemed to have less control over what students were learning than my initial training had led me to expect. I began asking myself questions – some more explicitly than others – such as:

- Why is it that what my students learn doesn't more closely resemble what I teach?
- Should I spend so much time trying to achieve accurate grammar from my students?
- Should my lesson plan rule the proceedings?
- What is the most efficient way of improving students' performance, given they don't have a lot of time to learn the language?
- What can you really do for those 'intermediate plateau' students who need a breakthrough and a feeling of progression?
- What can you do for advanced students after they have met the third conditional? And what is 'advanced' English anyway?

I began an extended period of extra study free from the constraints of day-to-day lesson planning and thinking about my particular students. This allowed me to stop being preoccupied with my teaching for a while and as a result, I found myself drawn more and more to considering the nature of language itself and the nature of language learning – what the process in which I was engaged and for which I was trained was really all about. Surprisingly, my initial training had not included study of this at all. It was concerned exclusively with how the teacher should teach; learners and learning were hardly discussed at all.

TASK

What percentage of the time in your training was spent looking at teaching and what percentage was devoted to learning?
After a lesson now, do you tend to think mostly about what **you** did, or about the learners?

I very soon came to two broad conclusions. Firstly, there was no guarantee that learners learn what teachers teach. Secondly, the grammar/vocabulary dichotomy was spurious, and the central role of grammar, at least as defined within my training, probably needed to be re-evaluated.

Making slight methodological changes in the light of these conclusions would not have satisfied me. I needed to get below the surface, explore the theory which lies behind classroom procedures, and decide what the real implications for the classroom could be. Let me explain in more detail how I came to these conclusions and show how they relate to the importance of teaching collocation in the classroom.

1.2 Learners don't learn what teachers teach

Although it is hard for many teachers to accept, it simply is not true that our students necessarily learn what we teach them. Teaching is, on the whole, organised, linear and systematic, but it is a mistake to think that learning is the same. Learning is complex and non-linear, and although the result may be a system, its acquisition is far from systematic. We cannot control what students learn, in what order they will learn and how fast they will learn. As Diana Larsen-Freeman writes in a disconcerting footnote to an article in the journal *Applied Linguistics:* 'I am constantly reminding students, audiences and myself that teaching does not cause learning.'

This has had an important implication for the way I teach: I no longer expect students to master an item or items of language before exposing them to more. Expecting mastery in the immediate short term is an unrealistic expectation. The fact is, they may or may not acquire what you teach them. If they do, they may acquire it immediately, later or only partially.

TASK
Should learners more or less master one new item or area before being exposed to more, or are you happy introducing new points even if learners may, in the short term, find this more confusing?

What has this to do with teaching collocation? Imagine a student produces *He's a strong smoker.* You could simply supply the student with the standard collocate – *heavy* – and move on. But an ideal opportunity to activate language on the edge of the student's lexicon has been missed. It requires very little extra time or explaining to add: *occasional, chain* and *non* as more collocates of *smoker.* Given that you cannot know whether students will remember and use *heavy smoker,* you might as well give them three more. They might remember none, one, two of them or all of them. Adding collocation to your teaching by consciously introducing one or two new words and re-activating other half-known words in this way increases the chance of acquisition taking place, though you cannot be at all sure what the acquisition encouraged (but not 'caused') by this particular bit of teaching will be.

One of the questions I posed for myself after teaching for a number of years was the extent to which my lesson plan should dominate proceedings. These days, I am less concerned about achieving the language aims in my plan and more concerned about spotting and responding to opportunities like the *heavy/occasional/chain/non- smoker* scenario – whether prompted by a student error or finding a collocation in a text to which I can add a handful of other useful collocates. This mindset is perfectly captured by Peter Wilberg's discussion of responsibility in *One to One,* and quoted by Michael Lewis at the beginning of *The Lexical Approach*: "The teacher's main responsibility is response-ability."

TASK
How much control do you think you have over what your students learn?
Do you still try to follow your lesson plan fairly rigidly?
How willing are you to forget your plan and respond spontaneously with unprepared input?

1.3 Knowing a word is complicated

Related to the point that learners don't necessarily learn what we teach is the fact that teaching tends to be linear and step-by-step in nature, whereas learning is holistic, cyclical and evolves over time. This is because new input means individual learners constantly need to make adjustments to what they have already internalised. Learning is not simply additive; it involves the learner re-organising his or her previous interlanguage. For example, learners do not really understand the present perfect until they understand the present simple and the past simple too, and the relationships that the meanings of all these different verb forms have with each other. Tenses are not understood in isolation from each other and it follows that learners' understanding of a particular tense develops as they encounter different uses of that tense and see it used or not used in preference to, and in (implied) contrast with, other tenses.

The same principle of meeting new uses, and becoming more aware of 'negative' choices – choosing one item implies rejecting several similar alternatives – applies to items of vocabulary. Take the word *injury*. This word can be understood by a student from its dictionary definition and all will be fine until the student comes across the word *wound*. S(he) then has to re-assess what *injury* means in the light of the new discovery, a discovery the teacher may wish the learner had never made when the learner asks: *What's the difference between 'wound' and 'injury'?* One's instinct – and my initial training – leads you to answer such a question by trying to **define** the difference between pairs of this kind, but this only leads to problems and what are at best half-truths. The difference between the two does not lie in dictionary definitions but rather that we say, for example, *stab wound* not *stab injury*, and *internal injuries* not *internal wounds*. In other words, it is the **collocational fields** of the two words which reveal the difference of meaning, or rather more precisely, the difference between the ways the words are used.

TASK
Look at these pairs of words:

work / job
house / building
understand / realise

Can you define the difference between each pair?
Can you list a few collocates of each word in each pair? (You may want to look them up in a collocation dictionary or use a computer concordance program.)
Which do you think would help your learners more – the definitions or the lists of collocations?

From the classroom point of view, if learners are slowly but continually evolving their understanding of the target language, whether grammar or lexis, it follows that giving students collocations of words newly or previously met will widen their understanding of what those words mean and, more importantly, how they are used. Taking a few minutes to supply these collocations in a lesson shortcuts the process of building up meaning and therefore acquiring. If you do not actively introduce additional collocations, it may be weeks, months or years before students meet those collocations and therefore the process of evolving and deepening understanding is delayed. Actively introducing collocations recycles half-known words and, while this does not directly cause learning, it accelerates it.

Some teachers might say at this point that there is not enough time to explore the collocations of words in this way – there are too many other important things to do, particularly explaining things. A great deal of time is spent in many classrooms explaining what things mean. For the reasons above, I suggest that at least some of that time is better spent showing students what words do – how they are **actually used** and how they collocate – rather than explaining what they mean. Explaining **and** exploring is surely better than either alone.

TASK
Are you happy with the idea of explaining less and giving and discussing more examples instead?

1.4 The intermediate plateau

Referring to my earlier question: *What can you really do for those 'intermediate plateau' students who need a breakthrough?* A big part of the answer lies in the strategy just discussed. The reason so many students are not making any perceived progress is simply because they have not been trained to notice which words go with which. They may know quite a lot of individual words which they struggle to use, along with their grammatical knowledge, but they lack the ability to use those words in a range of collocations which pack more meaning into what they say or write. The answer lies in teachers continually bringing useful collocations to students' attention and helping them to remember them, rather than trying to improve their grammar or giving them a lot more new words, which can so easily mean obscure, rarely used words. Most intermediate students would improve dramatically if they spent less time trying to perfect their grammar and learn new, rare words, and instead simply learned to use the words they already know in the huge number of collocations of which these words are parts.

A shift in approach of this kind will almost certainly need to come initially from the teacher as (s)he trains students to re-direct their priorities in ways which are most likely to produce both perceived and genuine progress.

1.5 The grammar-vocabulary dichotomy is invalid

So much of language teaching over the years has been based on the dichotomy of grammar and vocabulary: master the grammar system, learn lots of words and then you will be able to talk about whatever you want. This view of language has meant that students have learned to name a lot of things – an extensive vocabulary, predominantly nouns – and then struggled to use grammar to talk about those things. No wonder students make so many grammar mistakes! They are using grammar to do what it was never meant to do. Grammar enables us to construct language when we are unable to find what we want ready-made in our mental lexicons. But so much of the language of the effective language user is already in prefabricated chunks, stored in their mental lexicons just waiting to be recalled for use.

These chunks of lexis, which include collocations, do more than just name things, they also have a pragmatic element. They enable you to talk about things – to 'do' things. This raises the status of collocation to much more than just 'words which go together'. Many collocations have immediate pragmatic force or are situationally evocative. For example, it is hard to think in which situation someone might say: *This is a corner*. But if I say to you: *This is a dangerous corner*, it immediately suggests two people in a car as they approach a corner where lots of accidents have happened. The collocation *dangerous corner* is immediately evocative of a situation or a speech event. Notice, it is not simply that an adjective has been added to the word *corner*. The item *dangerous corner* exists as a prefabricated chunk with its own sanctioned meaning. Taking it apart would do damage to what it does, even what it is. Therefore, what collocation has put together, let no teacher pull apart!

Language is full of such examples – two (or more) word collocations which express something specific in precisely the form in which they typically occur. Tampering with items of this kind in any way means they completely lose their communicative power. Although such items may be only two or three words, a great deal of meaning may be packed into them, so one of these items can evoke a complex situation very precisely.

TASK

What event, situation or topic does each of these collocations suggest:

widely available	*routine check-up*	*boost employment*
disperse the crowd	*catch up with the news*	

Are they typical of spoken English, newspapers, novels or what?

To me, they suggest: talking about a new product, a visit to the doctor or dentist, a government aim, police action after an incident, and friends who haven't spoken for a while. In the classroom, items such as these must be brought to students' attention and the bigger context they suggest must be shown. Once this has been done, it is safe to translate the item into the learners' mother tongue. Not word-for-word but whole phrase to whole phrase, bearing in mind that the structure of the expression may be very different in one language from the equivalent expression in the other.

There are two important points here. Firstly, if you do not teach collocations, you are ignoring a large set of items which express often complex ideas very simply and yet precisely. Secondly, the fewer collocations students are able to use, the more they have to use longer expressions with much more grammaticalisation to communicate something which a native speaker would express with a precise lexical phrase and correspondingly little grammar. Notice too, that if native speakers usually express an idea lexically with a collocation, the non-native speaker, not knowing the lexical item, has to use grammar to express the idea in a way which they have not heard in that context – they have no model to guide them. They are in uncharted territory, which further increases the chance of grammatical error. If the teacher is not careful, this can lead to more grammar explanations and practice when what is really needed is work to expand the learners' mental lexicons.

An example may make this clearer. The student who doesn't know the expression *adequate supplies to meet the demand* is forced to construct something like: *We don't have things enough so that every person who will have one can have one.* The message has, perhaps, been successfully communicated in this case but most teachers would probably feel obliged to step in and help. Anyone who has the collocations *adequate supplies, meet the demand*, as part of their mental lexicon is able to recall them as complete phrases. This means the more collocations learners have at their disposal, the less they need to grammaticalise. This in turn means more brainspace is available to generate and process content. Here are more examples of natural collocations and students' attempts to construct the same ideas:

Collocation	**Students' attempt**
set yourself a realistic objective	You must know what you want to do but it must not be too much for it to be possible for you to do.
cause insurmountable difficulties	make problems which you think have no answers
major turning point	a very important moment when things changed completely
revised edition	a new book which is very similar to the old one but improved and up-to-date

It is a major change of mindset for teachers to realise that many grammatical errors are caused by lexical deficiencies, and that the best response to many of these errors at intermediate and advanced levels is to do more lexical work in place of grammatical correction. It may, of course, be necessary to introduce this idea to learners and persuade them of the value of putting more emphasis on collocation and other lexical work.

1.6 Advanced English

I refer back to another of my earlier questions: *What can you do for advanced students after the third conditional? And what is 'advanced' English anyway?* Advanced students become frustrated when they are unable to talk or write about ideas which they can comfortably talk or write about in their mother tongue. More complicated or this-will-challenge-them grammatical structures do not help them to do this. Unfortunately, this has been the standard diet of many advanced materials, encouraging learners to produce such convoluted gems as: *Were I richer, I would definitely buy one* or *Had I not arrived in time, the kitchen would have caught fire.* The language which helps learners to communicate more complicated ideas is not convoluted grammar structures like these, but different kinds of multi-word phrases, particularly densely-packed noun phrases *(firm but relaxed parental discipline, modern cities in the developed world, the continuing decline of educational standards)* and adverbial phrases *(in marked contrast, referring back to my earlier point, later that year, in the late twentieth century).* As the first two adverbial examples show, among the most important phrases are those which create cohesion across written text. The important thing to note is that all these multi-word phrases are collocations of different kinds.

I no longer worry about how to challenge my advanced classes with obscure grammatical constructions or unusual words. I simply keep my eyes open when using a text for collocations which I can bring to their attention and which we can then explore together.

An important point to make is that very often the words in the collocations are not new or difficult at all. For example, the item, *a major turning point* does not include any individually difficult words for an advanced student but this very fact means that both teacher and student can too easily assume it is not worth their attention. In fact, it is often true to say that neither learners nor the teacher even **recognise** it as a new item, so an extremely useful collocation slips by unnoticed and is therefore unavailable for storage and re-use by the learners.

Asking students: *Are there any words you don't understand?* is, therefore, not a helpful question. They may indeed understand all the words but fail to notice the combinations those words are in. My questioning of students now goes more like this:

> T   Is there anything in the first paragraph you think you
>   should write in your notebooks? (silence while students
>   scan the paragraph) Nothing?
>
> SS   No.
>
> T   Are you sure? I don't believe you. (more silence and
>   looking) What about the expression with *risk*? In all my
>   time as a teacher I've never heard a student say or write
>   *run the risk of*. Perhaps my students have never noticed it.
>   Do you use this expression? (general shaking of heads)
>   Perhaps you have never noticed it either. OK, write it in
>   your notebooks, then.

Being more proactive in pointing out useful language and getting learners to record it is an essential role of the teacher. This goes against thinking which encourages a student-centred, exploration approach to language. While I agree that learners should take responsibility for their own learning, they should not be taking responsibility for choosing which language items are more linguistically useful. Interestingly, after a period of teacher-dominated instruction (I prefer to call it learner training) of the kind exemplified above, learners begin to notice more of this kind of language for themselves, and start asking me about items in text, thus becoming more autonomous in their approach. And the questions they ask are better. Better than me asking *Are there any words you don't know?*, better than them asking only *What does this word mean?* Students begin asking *Is this a common expression? What does this expression mean? Is this a collocation?* These questions represent a real improvement as they mean learners are now asking about language which they **hadn't even noticed before**.

I have found that higher level students sense very quickly that they are gaining useful ground when collocations are drawn to their attention in this way. Because they are being equipped to say or write more complicated ideas, a new sense of satisfaction, and therefore motivation, develops. [Deborah Petty makes the same point about her learners. See p 95. Ed]

1.7 Leave 'used' language alone

'Used' language is what David Brazil has evocatively called language which has already been used naturally in speech or writing. Although we call this language 'used', that is not to suggest that it has been in any way damaged or soiled in the process. Perhaps because of the preoccupation with grammar over the years, and the determination to find generative systems, used language, particularly speech, has often been thought to need a good clean up before it can form 'good' input. Once cleaned up, it has usually been broken down into individual words. Collocation has been ignored or at least under-valued because of this obsession with breaking down used language.

TASK

How do you encourage learners to record language in their notebooks?

Do you ask them to record examples **exactly** as they find them?

Do you 'clean the examples up' so that what learners record is similar to a dictionary entry?

Do you encourage them to write (or prevent them from writing) translations?

In order for collocation to assume its rightful place in the classroom, it is not enough to simply have an understanding of what it is and a sense that it can help learners increase their communicative power. There needs to be a conviction that we should leave as much language as possible **in the form in which we find it**. Avoid breaking it up; keep something of the context and keep the chunks which are recorded as large as possible. Avoid grammatical cleaning up, and remember attempting to generalise may result in you losing, not adding, relevant information about how the language is actually used.

Noting multi-word vocabulary in **exactly** the form it is found in text, recording it, and trying to remember it in that form for re-use later has been, at best, on the periphery of language teaching, when in fact it deserves a central role. [Michael Hoey discusses this point at some length, p 230. Ed]

Below are some examples of language which my learners recorded. They recorded some of them in the form in which they found them, so these are potentially re-usable if remembered. Others, despite my efforts to guide the learners, they recorded in a 'cleaned up' version, which means that if they are to be used again, the learners will have to manipulate the items before they can actually use them. It goes without saying that manipulation requires more processing time, and gives more opportunity for grammatical error, or using the language in an unnatural way. The left hand column is what the learners recorded; the right hand column is what I wish they had recorded, which is what actually occurred in the texts and dialogues from which the examples were taken:

Take the hint	*OK. I can take a hint.*
Follow in someone's footsteps	*He's following in his father's footsteps.*
Turn a blind eye	*I decided to turn a blind eye.*
To rule out the possibility of	*We can't rule out the possibility of +...ing*
Stand on your own two feet	*It's time you stood on your own two feet.*
On the other hand	*On the other hand*
It's not worth it.	*It's not worth it.*
I searched high and low for it.	*I searched high and low for it.*

Of these eight items, only the last three are recorded in the most useful way. I also suggest that because they have more context, they are more situationally evocative and they are, therefore, more likely to be remembered. They can also be translated more safely.

The argument has been advanced that learners can generalise from the traditional *to take one's time*, or *to give somebody a hand* but may not be able to generalise from the actually used examples: *Take your time, Can I give you a hand?* Such an argument is surely wholly illogical; the cleaned up infinitive versions are themselves neither more nor less than generalisations of the used examples. Used examples provide a perfectly adequate basis for other generalisations and have the added advantages of being both more memorable and more immediately usable.

Related to this idea of respecting used language is the fact that there are a lot of words in the lexicon that have very little precise meaning until they are actually used. For example, the meaning of *get* is impossible to pin down until it is used and has co-text. The important point is that it is most commonly used in relatively fixed expressions with collocations – *they're getting married, we got wet, we got thrown out, I've got a bad cold* and so on. Ignoring these expressions in the forms in which they occur, or taking them apart in order to establish the meaning of *get* is ridiculous, as the learners will only have to put them together again in order to use the original expressions. Once you have realised that the mental lexicon contains many multi-word chunks, as well as individual words, the teaching of collocations is inevitable if you wish to remain true to the subject matter you are teaching.

So, having laid a theoretical basis for collocation having a central role to play in the classroom, let us consider some practical ways this can be done.

1.8 Some classroom activities

1. Don't correct – collect

Knowing a noun allows you to name a concept, but this is a long way from being able to talk about the concept. So, a learner who makes a collocation mistake when trying to talk about something provides the ideal opportunity to expand and organise the learner's lexicon in a very efficient way, similar to the *strong smoker* example discussed earlier. Don't just correct the mistake, give some extra collocations as well – three or four for the price of one. The transcript below shows how this works.

S	I have to make an exam in the summer.
	(T indicates mistake by facial expression)
S	I have to make an exam.
T	*(Writes 'exam' on the board)*
	What verb do we usually use with 'exam'?
S2	Take.
T	Yes, that's right. *(Writes 'take' on board)*
	What other verbs do we use with 'exam'?
S2	Pass.

T   Yes. And the opposite?
S   Fail.
T   Yes.
     (Writes 'pass' and 'fail' on the board)
     And if you fail an exam sometimes you can do it again.
     What's the verb for that? *(Waits for response)*
     No? OK, re-take. You can re-take an exam.
     (Writes 're-take' on the board)
     If you pass an exam with no problems, what can you say? I
     passed . . .
S2   Easily.
T   Yes, or we often say 'comfortably'. I passed comfortably.
     What about if you get 51% and the pass mark is 50%?
     What can you say? I . . . *(Waits for response)*
     No? I just passed. You can also just fail. *(Writes on the board)*

For advanced learners you may also give them *scrape through*. I use formats similar to this to organise the responses:

take	
re-take	
pass	an exam
fail	
scrape through	

With this language, students can not only **name** the concept *exam*, they have the collocations they need to **talk about** exams with confidence.

TASK

You may like to think how you would respond if a learner said one of these in your class:
I am too fat so I have to make a strong diet.
If you have a problem with yourself it is good to talk about it in an open way to a near friend.
Everybody must agree with the law if we want a good society.
Which nouns are you going to explore? What questions will you ask to elicit or teach extra collocations?

You can extend this activity further by thinking not only of collocates of the main word in question, but also of other common collocations and expressions likely to be said or written around the same topic. In the *heavy smoker* example it is only a very short step to elicit or give the item *give up smoking*. And from there you could add: *I wish I could give up smoking*. Suddenly you find yourself with two minutes practice of *I wish I could . . .* as you elicit other vices from your students. All this from responding to a collocation error and thinking aloud and so stimulating the class to ask: *What else do we say when talking about smokers and smoking?*

2. Make learners be more precise

It is obviously demotivating if every time students communicate effectively, the teacher nitpicks and asks for perfection. However, at the right time and in the right way, improving students' performance is an important part of the teacher's job, and what students need. So, if a student produces: *I was very disappointed*, point out the options: *bitterly/deeply disappointed*. Or if a student writes: *There are good possibilities for improving your job*, you may want to write *excellent promotion prospects* in the margin. In other words, it's not just mistakes that are opportunities for teaching but also the kind of circumlocutions we discussed earlier. If you notice the roundabout expressions which are the symptom of the lack of the necessary lexis, you will frequently recognise opportunities for helping students be more precise or more concise.

3. Don't explain – explore

When students ask *What's the difference between . . .* , for two words of similar meaning such as *wound/injury* discussed earlier, rather than spending too much time explaining the difference, give three or four contextualised examples of each word – that is, provide the appropriate collocational language. For example, with *make* and *do* you might give: *make a mistake, make an enquiry, make the most of the opportunity; do your best, do some overtime, Can you do me a favour?* and so on. The same procedure is particularly useful with those nouns which have very little meaning unless used in collocations, such as: *effect, position, action, point, way, ground.* (If you look in a collocation dictionary, you will see that these nouns have very large collocational fields. The most important part of 'knowing' a word like this is knowing a large number of its collocations.) Consider this classroom scenario:

T   . . . yes, that's a good point, Marco.

S   Excuse me but you said 'point' again. You say it in every
lesson but it's sometimes different. What does 'point'
mean?

T   Point . . . well, we use it in different ways, and it's very
common. Here are some typical ways we use it.
(Writes on the board):
Why do you want me to do that? I can't see the point;
*I know you want to come but, the point is, you're not old
enough.*
That's a good point. I hadn't thought of that.
I always make a point of saying thank you to the bus driver.

> It's difficult to say exactly what *point* means but you
> could learn these expressions and there are lots more so
> let's see if we can collect more. If you hear me use one,
> stop me and we'll write it with the others. If you meet one
> outside the class, write it down and tell us at the next
> class. When you look at them later, try to think what
> expressions you would use in Italian to express the same
> ideas. Check with Paola or another Italian speaker to see
> if you agree.

Although possibly more time-consuming than an explanation of *point*, surely meeting four typical uses is time better spent than trying to get to grips with what would have to be a vague, complicated and ultimately unhelpful definition.

4. If in doubt, point them out

One of the reasons students have not learned collocations is simply because teachers have not pointed them out in the texts they are using. This happens sometimes because the teacher's approach to dealing with the vocabulary in the text is to ask the class: *Are there any words you don't know?*

Collocations are missed with this approach because the words of the collocations may not be new, but the fact they occur together, and are worth noticing and recording together, must be pointed out by the teacher if students are not to 'look straight through' language which will expand their mental lexicons. Peter Skehan (*A Cognitive Approach to Language Learning*) makes a similar point when he writes:

> In this view, the role of instruction is not necessarily therefore in
> the clarity or in the explanation it provides, but rather in the way it
> channels attention and brings into awareness what otherwise would
> have been missed.

Simple questions such as *What's the verb before 'opportunity' in the first paragraph?* draw students' attention to collocations. Once that has been done – let's say the verb was *miss* – quickly add some others: *take, grab, make the most of*, using the collection and recording technique discussed above.

Instead of asking questions, you can prepare a simple worksheet or use the board or overhead projector to list parts of the useful collocations in the text. I often do this while students are engaged in a more global reading task. They then have to go back and search the text for the missing parts of the collocations. For any collocations which are worth adding to, I elicit or give more very quickly. Do not assume students are noticing collocations and recording them for themselves. They won't unless you train them to. I have found that after a short period of time, students begin to ask me about collocations in texts – whether they are worth recording – and they also ask for extras because that is what they have learned to expect from me. [Jane Conzett also points out in her paper that students do begin to collect collocations for themselves, once they have been introduced to the idea. Ed].

5. Essay preparation – use collocation

Students sometimes complain that they lack ideas when sitting down to write a composition on a prescribed topic. Teachers complain that they do not want to spend half the class time telling students what to write. There is a simple answer. Many teachers brainstorm words connected with the topic in class before setting the composition for homework. When the words are on the board, the next step is to add, where possible, useful collocates to each word. It is particularly important to introduce the nouns which will be central to the content of the essay. As we saw with the *exam* example above, this provides students with language items with more communicative power than individual words can offer.

Also, as we saw earlier, collocations are much more situationally evocative and correspondingly far more likely, therefore, to spark the imagination for writing. A dictionary such as *The LTP Dictionary of Selected Collocations* is invaluable for selecting collocates. With a class set, I give the students eight key nouns central to the essay topic. For example, with an 'education' topic, I might give them: *school, education, qualification, teacher,* etc. I then ask them to look up these words in the dictionary and note down collocations for each of the words that catch their eye or which they think they might use. They might choose for *school: drop out of, leave, skip, go to, single-sex, mixed, state, private.* Draw their attention particularly to the importance of *verb + noun* collocations. If students have their own dictionary, they can do this at home.

When the written work comes in, I often find either collocation mistakes or cases where students have used simple or vague words when they could have used more specific or interesting ones. For example, if a student writes *very intelligent,* and *big mistake,* I write in the margin other options such as *highly intelligent* and *disastrous mistake,* or ask them to refer to the *Dictionary of Selected Collocations* to make their own selection before rewriting their work with the improvements.

6. Make the most of what students already know

Some students already know a lot of 'simple' words but are not aware of what those words can do for them because they haven't noticed their common collocations. I regularly take such words, usually nouns, and brainstorm adjectives and verbs which students think go with those nouns. Very often, these collocations are already half-known by students – they sense they have met them before – but they have not yet internalised them. Time spent on half-known language is more likely to encourage input to become intake than time spent on completely new input. Again, Skehan suggests that ". . . very often the pedagogic challenge is not to focus on the brand new, but instead to make accessible the relatively new".

> **TASK**
> Do you think it is better to teach learners a lot of new words, or to extend their knowledge of some of the words they already half-know? Is your answer different for learners at different levels?

For example, I take the word *situation* and ask students to give me first adjectives and then verbs which they think collocate. The number they give me is usually very small, even for advanced classes. I then supply extras, perhaps: *awkward, complicated, critical, desperate, farcical; accept, analyse, assess, be in command of, make the best of the* etc. Again, a dictionary of collocations is a very useful resource for this kind of systematic expansion of students' mental lexicons. If you want to, you can ask follow-up questions such as: *Can you remember the last awkward/farcical/desperate situation you were in? Do you always analyse situations or do you just accept them?* Because so many collocations are situationally evocative, students often find they have something to say in response to these questions – something is triggered because collocations evoke bigger speech events than individual words usually do.

Note that it is better to ask questions with *or* rather than simple *Yes/No*-questions because they elicit more language in response. *Or*-questions also create an opportunity for the collocations to be used immediately. Typical questions are: *Do you sometimes break promises or do you always keep them? Do you always come by bus or do you sometimes come by car? Have you got a challenging job or a cushy job?* I must emphasise, however, that I do not see it as very important that students actually use the collocation there and then. From the point of view of acquisition, I would rather spend time adding more useful collocations to the noun than spend too much time in laborious practice of fewer items.

> **TASK**
> What percentage of the 'new vocabulary' you present in a lesson do you expect your learners to acquire from that lesson?
> Do you think your expectation is realistic?

I do not expect students to remember or acquire all or even the majority of language I expose them to. But for the reasons discussed earlier in this paper, I believe exposing students to more increases the chances of **some** acquisition taking place. Recently, I was observed teaching in this way by some teachers on a refresher course. At the end of the lesson with the board full of collocations, one teacher remarked: *It would be a miracle if they remembered*

50% of what you teach them. I replied, *It would be a miracle if they remembered 10% of what I presented.* We discussed the difference in our views at some length but I suspect he remained unconvinced. We simply had different mindsets. The teacher in question apparently believed that step-by-step teaching produces step-by-step learning, even mastery of what was presented. Both research and reflection on classroom experience show that this simply is not the case. Students do not have enough time to find that out for themselves; it is our job to provide the most effective learning based on our professional understanding of both language and learning.

7. Record and recycle

It is becoming clear that the lexicon is much bigger than anyone previously thought. This implies a greater memory load, an increased learning load – or certainly an increased input load – and this being the case, careful and systematic recording of collocations which ensures accurate noticing of useful language is essential. During class time, I encourage students to write down collocations in their main note-taking books and ask them to transfer them later into the collocation section of their lexical notebooks using formats such as the one shown earlier. As much as possible, I encourage students to record collocations in topic groups.

I use a simple and time-efficient approach to recycle collocations. Before the lesson, I make a list of all the collocations I want to recycle but delete part of each collocation before photocopying the list for each student. Students then search their notebooks to fill in the missing part of the collocation. If the collocations came from the same text, I sometimes ask students to re-construct the main content of the text, or parts of the text, using the collocations as prompts. This activity has the added usefulness of encouraging and including those students who may have trouble answering comprehension questions about the text for linguistic reasons but who are able to participate by remembering parts of it, however falteringly.

One important point: when deciding which part of the collocation to delete, leave the word or words which most strongly suggest what the missing part is. For example, for the collocation *a window of opportunity*, it would be better to delete *opportunity*, as *a window of . . . . .* is more helpful than *. . . . . opportunity.* Your choice of deletion, therefore, is a principled one with the aim of **helping** learners to remember, not trying to make the task artificially difficult.

A slight variation is to dictate part of the collocation and students have to remember or find the missing part in their notebooks before I dictate the whole item.

Other ways of recycling include: domino-type games – match the cards end to end by matching the collocations; 'find your partner' activities where two-word collocations are split between members of the class who then have to find their 'partner'; or a simple memory game with cards placed face down on the table and, in groups, students take it in turns to turn over two cards at a time hoping to find the collocations. A helpful principle to work with for recycling is little and often, with some variation.

1.9 Action research

All of these ideas can be incorporated painlessly into most teachers' current practice to a greater or lesser degree. Your teaching does not need to be turned upside down to make room for collocation. If, however, you are sceptical, why not allow yourself a trial period over the next few weeks to regularly incorporate some of the ideas into your lessons? Then take a moment to reflect on the effectiveness of the ideas and activities or even ask the class whether they have found the input helpful – a simple, step-by-step form of action research. A thoughtful evolution is more likely to be beneficial than a reckless or impatient revolution.

1.10 Conclusion

For many teachers, collocation is just another way of presenting vocabulary, and perhaps once every other unit of the coursebook, an exercise on two-word collocations appears and it is seen as a welcome change to the regular vocabulary building that goes on. Indeed, that is how I saw it up until about three years ago – useful, but peripheral. Teachers who do not stop to consider, or fail to grasp, the theoretical basis behind the teaching of collocation will only play at introducing it into the classroom. There will be no deep commitment to giving it a prominent role – the old arguments will crowd it out: *There isn't enough time to explain everything. There won't be enough time to practise. They won't remember all that. They still can't do the present perfect!* However, if we take a deeper look at the non-linear, unpredictable and holistic nature of learning, the nature of natural language – the way it is organised, the way it is stored in, and recalled from, the mental lexicon – collocation will become so central to everyday teaching that we will wonder whatever took up so much of our time before.

Discussion Questions

In what ways can you help learners on the intermediate plateau to gain a feeling of progress?

What do you do when your learners express themselves in roundabout, grammatically flawed ways? Do you think first of building their lexicons or correcting their grammar?

Chapter 2

Collocation – encouraging learner independence

George Woolard

George Woolard describes activities he uses which encourage learners to make the best use, from a learning point of view, of language which they meet outside the classroom. He encourages learners to take responsibility for their own learning, and uses part of the time in class to give his learners a real understanding of techniques for searching a text, dictionary, corpus or computer concordance in ways which help them expand their mental lexicons efficiently, even without the presence of a teacher. He discusses the importance of searching for and recording certain types of collocation which are particularly useful to learners. Throughout the chapter, readers may like to reflect on whether George's experience mirrors their own, and whether they are happy with the increasing emphasis George places on collocation in his classes.

2.1 Introduction

In recent years collocation has emerged as an important category of lexical patterning and it is fast becoming an established unit of description in language teaching courses and materials. The following is a personal account of how I have brought collocations into my classroom and how my teaching has undergone small but significant changes as a result.

I believe that the arbitrary nature of collocation is ideally suited to independent language learning and that we need to equip our students with skills to enable them to develop their knowledge of collocations independently of the teacher. This is particularly important in an age where technology has made large amounts of 'electronic' text readily available to our students through CD-ROM and the Internet.

I also recognise the importance of students recording the vocabulary they meet, and I outline a simple extension of the traditional vocabulary notebook to accommodate collocations and other co-textual patterns.

2.2 Collocation

As teachers, it is often instructive to remind ourselves that language teaching is, in its most basic form, a process of matching meaning with linguistic pattern. Language teaching courses and materials tend to classify the dominant patterns under the traditional labels; grammar, function, and the non-literal meaning categories of idiom and phrasal verb.

In order to avoid possible confusion and even antagonism, I prefer to adopt a definition of collocation that does not overlap or clash with any of these established categories. For me collocation does not re-define or re-order what I teach, it simply extends and enriches it. Therefore, for teaching purposes, I feel we need a definition that confines itself to a level of patterning that has previously received no explicit focus in our classrooms. A number of overlapping definitions of collocation exist, many of which have at their core some sense of the 'co-occurrence' of words. A typical definition is 'words which are statistically much more likely to appear together than random chance suggests'. Unfortunately, as a teacher, I find this type of definition unhelpful. It is simply too abstract and general to guide my students' attention to specific elements of text in a clear and directed way. In response, I have adopted what I feel is a more transparent and practical definition which involves looking at the language from the point of view of my students. I now re-examine the content of the texts in my coursebooks and lessons and try to anticipate and highlight groups of words – collocations – which I think my students **will not expect** to find together. For example, I do not draw attention to the combinations *heavy furniture/loads,* whereas I do for combinations such as *heavy seas/smoker.* The reason being that I expect my students to naturally associate the quality of being heavy with objects, but not with the sea or a smoker. I reserve the term collocation, then, for those co-occurrences of words which I think my students will not expect to find together. These are also the combinations that I would not expect my students to produce in their free production of language.

I have also restricted the use of the term to relations between nouns, verbs, adjectives and adverbs only. This serves two useful purposes. First, it provides a very clear definition of collocation for students. They can easily see the type of pattern that is the focus of attention, and furthermore, that it is a new and different kind of focus on language. Secondly, it avoids overlap with traditional vocabulary exercises such as those of 'dependent prepositions'. This means that I do not label co-occurrences such as *guilty of, depend on, reason for* as collocations. My current textbook has already classified these patterns, and exercises exist in the book that focus on such co-occurrences.

TASK

What definition of collocation do you think is most suitable for your own classes?

Would you include any areas such as idioms or phrasal verbs, or do you think it is best to confine the term in the way just suggested?

The definition of collocation I have adopted is essentially a pedagogic definition. It took me a while before I felt I could see useful collocations in text with ease, which suggests that teachers and students need to invest time in both absorbing the concept, and practice in noticing useful collocations in text. Before I became focussed on collocation, I would look at a text, and typical of the ELT profession, isolate the major grammar patterns and any items of useful vocabulary almost automatically. Now I find that it is collocations that are first to spring out of the texts I read. It is very much a case of seeing more than you used to in a text.

2.3 Raising awareness of collocation

One obvious way of finding out which words our students do not expect to find together is through the mis-collocations they make in their production of language. It is a good idea to keep a record of these mis-collocations as you correct your students' essays so that you can bring them into the classroom at appropriate times to improve and extend vocabulary teaching.

An effective platform for raising awareness of collocation is to focus on a selection of your students' mis-collocations. At first I suggest you restrict your examples to *noun + verb, adjective + noun* mis-collocations. Brown (1994) cites the following as typical examples of the mis-collocations produced by his students: Biochemists are *making research* into the causes of AIDS. The result was an *extreme disappointment*. We'll *experience many costs*, and few *benefits will come*.

Note that all three sentences are grammatically sound – that is, the students' use of tense, aspect and subject/verb agreement is accurate. The students' choice of vocabulary is also appropriate, and as a result, if the individual words are known by the listener/reader, communication is effective. However, our 'slot and filler' approach to the teaching of grammar and vocabulary has not sensitised our students to the collocational constraints on word combinations. For instance, the first sentence should be: *Biochemists are doing research into the causes of AIDS*. This is an extremely common *verb + noun* mis-collocation in which the verbs *make* and *do* are used with inappropriate nouns. Interestingly, this particular *verb + noun* pattern has been recognised and given attention in most traditional EFL courses and coursebooks, so '*make* and *do*' collocations provide a useful starting point for introducing the notion of collocation to learners. It is important to get across to students at this stage that these relations are arbitrary – there is no reason why it should be *make a decision* rather than *do a decision*. We need to make them aware that this is simply the way we say things in English and that's that!

The problem with the second sentence lies in the use of *extreme*. The expression *(X) was extremely disappointing* is very common, so it is not surprising that the student produced the sentence above. It seems a likely transformation. However, *extreme* does not collocate with *disappointment*. The most likely collocates are *big, great* and *bitter*. It is important to recognise that the grammar transformation exercises we use in grammar teaching can encourage mis-collocation.

The third example is very much topic-specific: *benefits* and *costs* are keywords in the language of business. In the sentence above we would be looking for stronger collocates such as: *We'll **incur substantial** costs, and few benefits will **accrue**.*

Although many native speakers would not instantly make these modifications, those working in the business field would do so more readily, especially in written communication. This is an indication of how collocation is closely tied to particular subject areas and, to a certain extent, it could be argued that topic-specific collocations are a major defining aspect of these areas. It follows that language proficiency within science, medicine, and commerce will be determined to a large extent by the students' mastery of the common collocations particular to each field. This means that a focus on collocation must become a major priority in Business English and English for Academic Purposes courses.

To sum up, for many students learning more vocabulary simply means learning new words. By focussing our students' attention on mis-collocations we make them aware that **learning more vocabulary is not just learning new words, it is often learning familiar words in new combinations**. How, then, do we help the learner to develop their mental lexicons in this way?

2.4 Highlighting and teaching collocation

Teachers have a prominent role to play in helping the learner identify collocations in texts. The use of student mis-collocations of the type given by Brown above is one strategy but teachers need to adopt a more proactive approach. A description of how my teaching developed in this direction will, I hope, help.

I was using a reading comprehension text with a multi-lingual intermediate class when one of the students asked what the word *views* meant in the following: *She holds very strong views on marriage. She thinks everybody should be married in a church.* My initial response was to employ the standard techniques:

　synonymy: *views = opinions*
　paraphrase: *views = what you think of something*
　contextualisation: *I think it's wrong to kill animals. What are your views?*

However, rather than move on in the lesson, I found myself directing the students' attention to the surrounding **co-text**. An exploration of the left co-text highlighted useful relations of collocation; adjective + noun – *strong views*; verb + noun – *hold views*. This left the students with a useful 'chunk' of language – *to hold strong views* – rather than a single word.

When the exercises designed for the reading text were completed, I added a supplementary exercise aimed at activating this chunk:

Exercise

Look at this part of the text:

'She holds very strong views on marriage. She thinks everybody should be married in a church.'

Most people hold strong views on something. What about you? Write some sentences about yourself following the pattern,

Most people hold strong views on . . . . Personally, I think . . . . .

This exercise resulted in students producing personal opinions such as: *Most people hold strong views on smoking. Personally, I think cigarettes should be banned.* Note how such responses demonstrate that students tend to notice more patterning than that which is the focus of the exercises we give them. Here the *noun + preposition* pattern *views + on* has been noticed and used, as with the grammatical structure *I think X should be (done)*. This natural ability to notice pattern should not be underestimated, and is the basis for the development of the independent learning strategies that we need to develop in our students.

One immediate implication for teachers is that they should re-examine their coursebooks for collocation, adding exercises which focus explicitly on co-text and which draw the students' attention to significant *verb + noun*, *adjective + noun, verb + adverb* collocations. To return to the example above, the next time I used this particular reading text I added a number of short vocabulary tasks to the comprehension exercises that accompanied the text:

Find a verb and adjective in the text which collocates with the word *views*. Then complete the following sentence:

My father . . . . views on drinking and driving. He thinks that these drivers should be banned for life.

As Swan (1996) points out, vocabulary will not take care of itself. Students with limited time available for study will not learn high priority lexis if it is not **deliberately selected** and incorporated into learning materials. Collocations, then, must become part of that planned language input. However, the selection of keywords needs to be informed and this necessitates a greater awareness of the nature of lexis.

2.5 Choosing key words

Lexicalisation is to do with the amount of information a word carries and this is a useful spectrum to guide our selection of words to target for collocation searches. Words like *penicillin* are high-content words and as a result have few common collocates. Test this out by trying to think of adjectives which collocate with *penicillin*. Note how few come readily to mind. On the other hand, *drug* is less lexicalised and will have a much greater collocational field. Note how you can readily generate a number of *adjective + drug* collocations – *addictive/effective/fast-acting/powerful* etc.

As we move further along this spectrum and as the degree of lexicalisation decreases, we find some of the most common and useful nouns in the lexicon, e.g. *character, idea, plan, problem, situation, way* etc. Unfortunately, vocabulary books and vocabulary lessons tend to focus on the more lexicalised words rather than these less lexicalised words. This means that these common and useful nouns often do not receive the amount or type of attention they merit. For example, with the word *way*, common semi-fixed expressions containing useful collocations of the following sort are not highlighted: *The most effective way of (losing weight/falling asleep/etc) is... .*

A further problem lies in the way vocabulary is traditionally taught. Decontextualised learning of individual words such as translation may be adequate for high information words like *penicillin*, while paraphrase and/or contextualisation of more common words like *drug* are usually sufficient to carry the meaning of the term. In general, however, teachers should be wary of presenting uncollocated nouns to their students. They have to become aware of the need to incorporate co-textual information into their teaching, especially with these less lexicalised items. As Lewis (1997) notes and argues:

> The real definition of a word is a combination of its referential meaning and its collocational field.

> In general, the more de-lexicalised a word is, and the wider its collocational range, the more important it is to meet, acquire and record it in a collocation.

In selecting vocabulary items from texts, teachers must develop their awareness of the differing degrees of lexicalisation of words and recognise that different types of vocabulary may need differing degrees of co-textual reference, and therefore, different teaching techniques. Teachers also need to develop their students' sensitivity to this spectrum of lexicalisation, and provide practice in separating nouns into high-content items and less lexicalised items, so that students focus their co-textual searches on the more common and useful items in the texts they meet, for example, words like *drug* rather than *penicillin, tool* rather than *wrench*. [See also pp 143/4]

Technical texts are useful for this purpose as the high-information items are easily identified by students, leaving them to explore the collocates of the less lexicalised keywords in these texts. Instruction leaflets and operating manuals are excellent sources of material for encouraging this awareness. As teachers, we need to prioritise the development of this kind of lexical sensitivity for all our learners.

2.6 The independent learner and learning strategies

A major problem remains over the amount of language that can be covered in the classroom. This will almost always be less than the student meets or needs. What is essential is that the teacher equips the students with search skills which will enable them to discover significant collocations for themselves, in both the language they meet in the classroom and, more importantly, in the language they meet outside the classroom.

We need to remind ourselves that collocation is mostly an arbitrary pairing of words. We can say *treat the patient, repair the damage,* but not *repair the patient, treat the damage.* It is a fact that much of the grammatically accurate language that we **could** use, is in fact **not** used. As teachers, then, we can offer no explanations to our students for the particular choices that are selected and sanctioned by the speech community, beyond saying 'this is simply the way the language is'. We should resist the teacher's automatic reflex of seeking explanations for all aspects of language patterning; to try, for example, to explain the fact that *repair* does not collocate with *patient* by looking for subtle semantic differences between the verbs *treat* and *repair.*

TASK

Do you think you can define the difference between the verbs *treat* and *repair*?

Here are some authentic examples from a computer concordance (see below) of the two verbs *repair* and *treat*:

One child was able to *repair engines* without being instructed.
He has had to work hard to *repair his* damaged *reputation*.
The natural tendency of *the body* is to *repair itself* given the opportunity.
It will take years to *repair the economic damage* caused by this policy.
Some dentists claim it is uneconomic to *treat* NHS *patients*.
In my profession, you learn how to *treat* your own *wounds*.
It is one of the few drugs approved to *treat Alzheimer's disease*.
Can you advise me on how to *treat the problem*?
You can *treat* tired, lifeless *hair* with this new shampoo.
They have a tendency to *treat* small *customers with contempt*.
It was no way to *treat a dog*.
We took *the dog* to the vet but he said it was too late to *treat* her.

Notice that two of the concordance examples – *treat customers with contempt, no way to treat a dog* – could confuse as they contain examples of *treat* with a different meaning. If you use unedited concordances, problems such as this frequently arise. While this can be helpful for more advanced learners, it strongly suggests that examples should be carefully selected for intermediate learners, although not selected to conform to a preconceived pattern. Notice particularly, the example *The natural tendency of the body to repair itself,* which immediately invalidates the apparently attractive 'treat people, repair machines' rule.

Almost always, a list of authentic examples makes you aware of both patterns and problems which you would have almost certainly overlooked if you had relied only on your intuition. Collocation is more varied than we tend to think, and looking at authentic examples will nearly always be more revealing than seeking an explanation based on subtle semantic differences.

One important implication of the arbitrary nature of collocation is that, apart from selecting and listing collocations, the role of the teacher is a relatively minor one. It is very much a case of being in 'telling' rather than 'teaching' mode. As such, the learning of collocations is one aspect of language development which is ideally suited to independent language learning. In a very real sense, we can teach our students to tell themselves. Collocation is mostly a matter of noticing and recording, and trained students should be able to explore texts for themselves. Not only should they **notice** common collocations in the texts they meet, but more importantly, they should **select** those collocations which are crucial to their particular needs. This is very much in line with modern trends in language teaching, where there is a shift from simply teaching the language to helping learners develop their learning skills. How, then, can we encourage and develop the students' ability to notice the collocations which are significant and useful for them?

I believe most students need to spend some time initially in identifying the basic grammar categories of noun, verb, adjective, and adverb, as these are the categories which are the focus of co-textual search strategies for collocation. This can be done through traditional exercises in sentence analysis. The next stage is to highlight the pivotal role of the noun. The fact that nouns tend to be the focus of information in a text, that we tend to build the information up around the nouns, means that they are the most suitable headwords for collocation searches.

Search strategies themselves are relatively simple and straightforward, and reflect the procedures we followed in teaching collocation above. We encourage the student to follow the steps below, and through practice make them routine and automatic:

1. Isolate key nouns in the text
2. Look for (unexpected) verb collocates
3. Look for (unexpected) adjective collocates
4. Look for (unexpected) adverb collocates

I've added 'unexpected' in brackets as a reminder that the purpose of these search strategies is **not** to notice **all** collocates of a word, but for learners to **select** those combinations that they do not already know or expect. For example, the collocation *big disappointment* is not surprising or unexpected whereas *bitter disappointment* is likely to be, which makes the latter worth noticing and recording.

We need, therefore, to actively encourage the development of these skills and give them sufficient focus in the classroom. One useful way of monitoring their development is to establish regular slots in the course programme where students report back to the class on interesting collocations they have encountered and noticed outside the classroom. It is probably true to say that the teacher's role today is becoming more and more one of facilitating learning, and one issue of importance centres on how we help our students maximise their learning of collocation outside the classroom.

2.7 Resources: dictionaries

A particular word may interest or be important to a student, who will naturally want to explore its collocational field further. However, if encounters with particular words are left to random or chance meetings in texts, learning will be extremely haphazard and inefficient. To a certain extent, we can partially resolve this situation by heeding Swan's earlier point that we provide a more concentrated exposure to collocations through careful planning of the vocabulary input to our courses. However, outside the classroom we need to direct our students to concentrated sources of this kind of information.

1. Traditional dictionaries

One would expect dictionaries to be an obvious source of relevant information. However, dictionaries tend to focus on the decoding process. That is, they provide excellent descriptions of the meaning(s) of words through synonymy and other word relations such as paraphrase and contextualisation. The organisation reflects the students' approach to the dictionary as a resource for answering the question *What does X mean?* A major drawback is that most dictionaries give relatively little explicit attention to collocation and other co-textual features of words.

Dictionaries can, however, be approached in a different way and prove to be a worthwhile source of information on collocation. A good English-English dictionary usually provides one or two expressions or sentences demonstrating the use of a word, and these will probably contain one or two useful collocates of that word. Teachers should encourage students to browse these examples for collocations. This needs to become an automatic habit.

By switching the focus to the collocational field of a word, the student is now using the dictionary as an encoding tool, rather than a decoding one. For most students this is new, and as such, they will need some guidance and training in using the dictionary in this way. An approach which I find useful, is to set exercises which actively direct the students to the dictionary to explore a word's collocates rather than its meaning. Such exercises can be free-standing or integrated into a lesson.

In one of my classes, the word *criticism* in the sentence *The Government has received heavy criticism for increasing taxes* became a focus. After dealing with the meaning and highlighting the collocates *receive* and *heavy*, I asked the students to look up *criticism* in their English-English dictionaries for homework. The idea was to see if they could find other verbs and adjectives which would complete the sentence, *The Government has . . . . criticism for increasing taxes*. The relevant entry in the COBUILD dictionary is:

> **criticism** 1. **Criticism** is the expression of disapproval of someone or something, by stating an opinion on their faults, weaknesses, or disadvantages in speech or writing. EG. *The Government came in for severe criticism. Some fierce public criticism of the plan had been voiced.*

From the two instances of use given by the dictionary the students were able to work out that the phrasal verb *come in for* could replace *receive,* and that *severe* and *fierce* were appropriate alternatives to *heavy.* This kind of noticing is vital to encoding and enables students to transfer their findings into their own production.

I then asked the class to talk about the criticism that their governments had met, and this led to a number of responses with the pattern, *My Government has come in for severe criticism for . . . .*

One obvious limitation of this approach lies in the rather small amount of language presented by the dictionary. This is certainly a problem if the student is looking for a particular collocation. More often than not, the dictionary will not provide it. [See also p 200] For example, some of my students attempting the task above felt that the criticisms of their governments weren't *heavy,* and wanted to know the contextual opposite of *heavy.* We had earlier noted that the opposite of *heavy cold* was *slight cold,* not *light cold.* The students' growing sensitivity to collocation had made them aware that one cannot assume that simple oppositions between adjectives such as *heavy/light, old/new* will work in all contexts.

2. Electronic dictionaries

What is clear is that dictionary entries in their present format cannot provide students with a sufficient range of collocates. Ideally, our students need a greater number of examples of use to browse. Fortunately, a number of solutions are becoming available through developments in computer technology. One of the easiest to use and understand is the 'electronic dictionary'. Most of the major ELT dictionaries are now available on CD-ROM, which allows the contents of the dictionary to be accessed and searched using a personal computer. The main advantage of the electronic format over the book format lies in the powerful and speedy search functions that the former has built into it. For example, the CD-ROM version of the *Oxford Advanced Learners Dictionary* has a full text search function which can be configured to search all the examples of use in the dictionary for a particular word or phrase. When I asked the dictionary to display all the examples of use which contained *criticism*, I was presented with about a hundred sample phrases or sentences, all of which could usefully be browsed for collocations. The richness of the information available is clearly shown by this selection:

> The new play has *attracted considerable criticism*.
> The head teacher *came under* a lot of *criticism* from the parents.
> There was *growing criticism* of the government's conduct of the war.
> I'm sick to death of your *endless criticism*.
> She *received* a lot of *unjustified criticism*.

The power and speed of the electronic medium in providing a larger sample of examples of use to browse for collocation means that, in order to promote and assist the independent learning of collocation, we need to make this type of resource available to our students and train them in the constructive use of their powerful search tools.

3. Collocation dictionaries

A further resource has appeared recently in the form of dictionaries of collocations. These dictionaries deal exclusively with co-text and provide a much more comprehensive account of a word's collocates than the traditional dictionary. Used in tandem with a traditional dictionary they help to provide some of the co-textual information that the former lacks.

The LTP Dictionary of Selected Collocations presents a range of common collocates of words in a clear and concise manner. Here is the entry for *criticism*:

> **CRITICISM**
> V: accept, agree with, answer, arouse, attract, be discouraged by/exposed to/impervious to/rattled by/subjected to/upset by, blunt, come in for/under/up against, crush, defend oneself against, deflect, deserve, encounter, escape, evoke, express, forestall, give rise to, ignore, invalidate, justify, level ~ against sb, meet with, offer, overcome, provoke, react to, reject, reply to, rise above, run into, shrink from, silence, soften, stifle, subject sb to, suffer, voice, weather, withstand, yield to ~
> V: ~ centres on sth, comes from sb, died down, grew, hardened, hit home, is relevant, mounted, revolved around ...
> A: adverse, basic, biased, bitter, blunt, common, constant, destructive, devastating, (un)fair, ferocious, fierce, friendly, fundamental, furious, harsh, helpful, hostile, implicit, incisive, lively, merciless, mild, muted, objective, oblique, open, overt, penetrating, perceptive, personal, savage, searing, severe, sharp, sincere, stinging, stringent, strong, subjective, tough, trenchant, unjust, unprecedented, useful, useless, (thinly) veiled, widespread ~
> P: chorus of, flood of, spate of, torrent of, wave of, whiff of ~

The entry uses the following system:

> V: verbs which come before the noun
> V: ~ verbs which usually come after the noun
> A: adjectives
> P: phrases which contain the noun

Intelligent browsing of this kind of resource can both guide and enrich the students' production of language. My students have found this to be an invaluable resource to have on hand when writing.

It is becoming clear that dictionaries are underused resources in language teaching and that they must be given a greater and more central role to play in language learning. In particular, browsing the exemplifying expressions and sentences in dictionaries can provide useful information on collocation, and teachers need to encourage and train their students to approach dictionaries in this way. I now encourage all my students to invest in a good English-English dictionary **and** a dictionary of collocations.

2.8 Resources: corpora and concordancers

Vast amounts of text are now stored on computers and many of the major English Language Teaching publishing houses and universities have established extensive banks of English or corpora. These are being constantly added to and updated. Some contain over 500 million words of both written and spoken text. These huge banks of data provide a basis for research into the use of English, and are used as a basis for modern dictionaries and teaching materials. Some of these large banks of English can now be accessed by individuals.

The recent development of the Internet and the World Wide Web has greatly increased the amount and diversity of 'electronic' English that can be accessed with comparative ease by individuals anywhere in the world. Today's students of English in non-English speaking environments are no longer restricted to the limited amount of language provided by the coursebook and classroom. They now have an endless amount of real English to explore and exploit. The question arises as to how they can use this wealth of text constructively, without being overwhelmed by the sheer amount or density of the information. A great deal of thought and development is going on in this area at the moment, but with our present concerns in mind, I would like to focus on one activity, that of 'concordancing', and how I have used it to help my students develop their knowledge of collocations.

A concordancer is a relatively simple piece of computer software which allows a constructive search of large amounts of text for examples of a particular word or phrase. Below is an edited example of a concordance produced for the word *disappointment*. Note how:

- the searchword *disappointment* is placed in the middle of the page where it is easily seen.
- only a single line of text is listed for each example and these are usually not complete sentences.
- the list is ordered alphabetically in some way. In the example below the word to the left is the focus of organisation. This makes searching much easier.

```
the decision will come as a disappointment to    development   agencies
an's Australia. He accepted disappointment and   defeat   with   dignity
n's absence would be a big  disappointment for   Spurs   as   his   fellow
in New York said: 'The big  disappointment was   exports.   Given   that
ter read wedge. <p> His big disappointment in    the   Ryder   Cup   was
oviding perhaps the biggest disappointment.<p>   That   race   went   to
failure is accompanied by   disappointment at    one's   own   incompetence
and had to admit, contained disappointment at    what   Himmler   had   to   sa
by Mikhail Gorbachev a deep disappointment to    his   countrymen   when
laughing and had expressed  disappointment that  they had not even he
several delegates expressed disappointment at    the  delay  in  the  elect
man's antics, but also from disappointment over   the   Chancellor   of
wers to be granted. Further disappointment arose  from  De  Klerk's  pr
Stewart's book is a great   disappointment.His  method is unchallenged
 made little secret of her  disappointment in the course of her husband
ling that goes with this is disappointment and    frustration.   <item>
```

Concordances provide much richer sources of co-textual information than dictionaries, and they can lead to a more efficient exploration of the collocates of a word. As with the dictionary, students will need time and training in how to do this constructively. Simple exercises which familiarise the students with the material and format are essential. For example, I presented my students with this frame and asked them to suggest ways of completing it: *I got grade E for Mathematics. The result was a . . . . disappointment.* Next I asked them to explore the concordance extract above, and they were able to extract *big, deep* and *great* as appropriate collocates for *disappointment.*

As students work through more and more exercises on collocation, they become more and more sensitive as to whether two words are possible collocates or not. Such sensitivity is particularly important for their own production.

For example, one student of mine had written the sentence: *I think there's a big possibility of rain today,* but expressed doubt about the collocation *big possibility.* Rather than just answer his question we ran a concordance for the phrase *big + possibility* and found no examples, suggesting that this combination if not impossible, is at least unlikely. It is important to recognise that it is not useful or appropriate to say it is a wrong collocation. We only searched a corpus of 2 million words, consisting mainly of newspaper articles, and a search of a larger and more varied corpus might well reveal an example of *big possibility.*

The purpose of the search is to uncover **probable** language, and my role as teacher is to show students how to find this for themselves, so that they will have the confidence to decide on their own, not 'whether something exists' or not, but whether it is probable. Decisions about collocation are about degrees of likelihood, not certainty.

This particular student then ran a concordance for *possibility* and noted a number of examples of *strong possibility* in the readout. As a result, he edited his own writing to *I think there's a strong possibility of rain today*. A large number of occurrences were taken as an indication of a common and therefore useful collocation. What is important to recognise in this process is that the student can search this type of data and make informed decisions, and that all this can take place without a teacher on hand.

Resources work best when their use is integrated, and concordances can and should be used intelligently with dictionaries. An example of the interplay between these two resources is exemplified by the same student. Below is an extract from the concordance output for *possibility* that the student explored.

```
the field, then it becomes a   possibility. The  manager  said  he   was
d make good progress.Another    possibility  is to let yourself off doing
they have also ruled out any    possibility  of supporting a rights issue
the recognition of the clear    possibility  that these increases in taxe
bery to consider the further    possibility  that learning might be excep
but there appeared to be no     possibility  of an early breakthrough.<p>
cly stated. The most obvious    possibility  is that the waning of the ov
ned by the value of Beta-One    possibility  advanced by Smith and Peters
on today are facing the real    possibility  of elimination as a people a
ly exist, albeit as a remote    possibility  in England, it is better alw
defeat was not even a remote    possibility. Money fell into his hands a
finally, there is the strong    possibility  that a contagion effect will
d that there is now a strong    possibility  of prosecutions being brough
refused even to discuss the     possibility  that she might be separated
fUR's action also raises the    possibility  of retaliation by other gove
o is a particularly worrying    possibility  and I urge everyone, Conserv
```

From these lines the student noted a number of instances of *remote possibility* and became interested in the word *remote*. After encouraging him to try to work out some of the word's sense from the concordance lines, I referred him to his dictionary, from which he was able to understand *remote possibility* as a contextual opposite for *strong possibility*.

Concordancing is a useful tool to employ in correction. There are times when directing the student to a concordancer is more constructive than simply making alterations to the student's text. I pointed out to the student who wrote the following: *We will have to increase our prices because of the increasing cost of advertising our products* that it contained *increase* and *increasing* and that it could be improved by changing one of these words. In response, the student ran a concordance on *cost + of* and, from the lines below, quickly found an alternative in *growing* and *rising*. Subsequent use of a dictionary would also allow the student to see possibilities in *mounting* and *spiralling*.

```
er, there was an exceptional    cost  of materials due to the staff reduc
savings to finance the extra    cost  of borrowing. <p> 'We are happy to
exposure to the fluctuating     cost  of money. <p> Called simple hedge
le awareness of the growing     cost  of high level scientific research,
The company blamed the high     cost  of computer memory chips and proble
Lipton singled out the high     cost  of computer memory chips, inventory
with the fact that the high     cost  of tunnelling raised doubt over cha
e space because of the huge     cost  of the railway works and decking t
 the Government to the huge     cost  of improving water quality. <p> Th
ncludes: (1) the increasing     cost  of technology, in terms of developm
ies shoulder the increasing     cost  of research and enable them to tend
orking capital. The initial     cost  of the franchise includes training.
ificed to meet the mounting     cost  of household bills. <p> The CBI fea
 frustrated with the rising     cost  of living, official corruption and
r Whit to escape the rising     cost  of the loan he took out to pick up
  uneconomic. The spiralling     cost  of both the tunnel itself and the
```

The increasing availability of vast banks of English stored on computer, coupled with a simple but powerful search tool like a concordancer empowers today's student. In particular, as we have noted, these resources are ideal for exploring collocation. It would seem essential, then, that all students should be trained to use a concordancer and given access to the wealth of English text that technology has made so easily available. Many teachers shy away from technology in the classroom, many also labour under the misconception that this kind of activity is an expensive and unnecessary luxury. I would argue that concordancing is an essential tool for effective independent learning, and add that the software and hardware requirements are relatively cheap. At the time of writing, concordancers like *Wordsmith* are available for well under £100 and they run on relatively small desktop computers. The programs are not complex and it only takes one short induction lesson to train students to use them for collocation searches.

It is worth adding here that a concordancer can be used to search any bank of electronic text. This means that it is possible to provide more efficient collocation searches by building up banks of text which match your students' needs. This is particularly useful for subject-specific courses like Business English, where teachers can build up a relevant bank of material by storing business letters, memos etc, on the hard disk of a computer. This is a fairly simple operation if the material is available as computer files, from CD-ROM, or downloads from relevant sites on the World Wide Web. If all of this is not possible, you can build up a less ambitious bank by the more laborious means of scanning text into the computer. Banks of material can also be graded for level to allow the less advanced student to concordance to good effect. Recently, I have started building up banks of material for elementary and intermediate students of English. Graded readers and General English coursebook materials are becoming increasingly available on CD-ROM and provide ideal sources for the creation of appropriately graded banks of text. Even the very elementary student can develop a degree of learner autonomy.

2.9 Lexical notebooks

There is more to the successful learning of vocabulary than simply noticing. It is important to record what is noticed in some way. We also know that a single encounter with a word is not enough to ensure its acquisition, and that subsequent encounters – research suggests a minimum of perhaps seven – are essential. Furthermore, it is now accepted that acquisition is facilitated by revisiting an item and recreating it in the production of language. All this points to the need to train our students to record, revisit and re-activate the significant vocabulary they meet. One simple tool for this purpose is the vocabulary notebook. A traditional way of recording vocabulary is in small notebooks. If these are to be helpful they need to be organised in some way. Many of my students keep notebooks organised alphabetically, devoting two or three pages to each letter. Some pages are also devoted to situations – *at the bank*; functions – *complaining*; and topics – *occupations*. I have modified the framework which I previously encouraged learners to use to record information about a word by adding two extra lines, as these examples show:

Previous format

CRITICISM
(pronunciation + translation)
to express disapproval of something or somebody
The government has received a lot of criticism for increasing taxes.

Revised format

CRITICISM
(pronunciation + translation)
to express disapproval of something or somebody
The government has received a lot of criticism for increasing taxes.
V: receive, come in for, ...
A: heavy, severe, fierce, ...

Verb and adjective collocates are recorded in a clear and compact format which has the advantage of taking up little extra space in the notebook.

It is important for both teachers and students to recognise that learning vocabulary is an ongoing and organic process. Items in the notebook are not just listed and left. They are revisited and extended in the light of the learners' increased exposure to the language. As such, I expect my students to add to their lists of collocates for *criticism* through subsequent encounters with the word. As their proficiency increases, their personal records incorporate more of the collocates listed under the entry *criticism*, cited earlier from the *LTP Dictionary of Selected Collocations*.

In a very real sense, a lexical notebook mirrors an individual's uniquely developing mental lexicon. More importantly, the notebook is not just a decoding tool, but a resource which individuals can use as an encoding instrument to guide their own production of language. Encouragement to use a notebook in this way should lead to fewer errors in their production. It is now clear that we need to give vocabulary notebooks a far greater priority in language teaching, and raise our students' awareness of the dynamic role they have to play in the process of learning a language. In order to give the expanded function and format of the notebook more prominence, it seemed appropriate to re-name it, and I now refer to vocabulary notebooks as lexical notebooks.

2.10 Word grammar

The definition of collocation that I have adopted in the classroom has a clear but fairly narrow focus. In the examples I cited earlier, the explorations of the words *views* and *criticism* were confined mainly to searches of the left co-text of occurrences of these words, and to relations between nouns, adjectives and verbs. However, as noted earlier, students can and do notice more, and we need to encourage further exploration of co-text. When I asked my students to look at the right co-text of *criticism* in the sentence *The government has received heavy criticism for increasing taxes*, they noted that *criticism* was followed by the preposition *for* and the *-ing* form of the verb. We summarised this information as . . . *criticism for raising taxes*. Subsequent encounters would obviously enrich the students' knowledge of other prepositions and verb patterns which occur with *criticism*. These patterns are traditionally associated with, and taught as, grammar, and I think it is appropriate to retain that association. However, I think there is a useful pedagogic distinction to be made between 'grammar' and what I have come to term 'word grammar'. The difference lies in the way we approach grammar patterns.

Traditional grammar teaching tends to operate on a slot-and-filler approach, with broad syntactic patterns such as the tenses as the primary focus. Lexis is a secondary consideration and fills the slots in the syntactic frames that define such patterns. A word grammar approach, on the other hand, **begins with the word**. Our orientation is one of moving out from the word to uncover the particular syntactic patterns associated with it. Consider the following combinations:

*The government has received a lot of criticism **for** its decision to raise taxes.*
*The government has received a lot of criticism **over** its decision to raise taxes.*
*The government has received a lot of criticism **for deciding** to raise taxes.*
*?The government has received a lot of criticism **over deciding** to raise taxes.*

The last two sentences follow the broad pattern of *noun + preposition + ...ing* form. However, most native speakers are uneasy with the final combination. Furthermore, I was unable to find a single example of this pattern in any of the large corpora I consulted. All this suggests that this particular pattern is improbable and therefore of no value to the learner.

Traditional grammar teaching allows the student to generate a large amount of grammatically accurate language, which is extremely important. However, as noted earlier, a lot of language which is grammatically accurate is not used, which is one reason for the large amount of improbable language our students produce. Grammar not only generalises, it often over-generalises. A word grammar approach complements the traditional approach to grammar by directing the students' attention to the syntactic constraints on the use of lexis. It directs the student towards probable language rather than possible language. Both approaches, then, are essential components of grammatical competence.

I now find it helpful to extend my own and my students' perception of what words are. I think it useful to see them as having, not just meaning, not just collocates, but also as having their own particular grammatical signatures. The small but significant changes this brings to my approach to teaching are neatly summarised by Michael Lewis when he suggests:

> Practice should be directed towards helping students collocate
> words and grammaticalise from words to sentences.

It is precisely this kind of practice that we need to prioritise and add to the established practices we employ in the classroom. It is very much a case of presenting our students with a richer picture of language patterning.

As with collocation, it is important that elements of word grammar are recorded in lexical notebooks. I suggest two further categories for entries in these notebooks, one (G) to record significant grammar patterns; the other (F) to record 'favourites', that is, patterns or expressions which the individual particularly likes and will probably use. This last category is important as we all have our own particular affinities for certain chunks of language. A personal entry for *criticism* in a lexical notebook might look something like this:

Current format for a learner notebook entry

CRITICISM
(pronunciation + translation)
to express disapproval of something or somebody
The government has received a lot of criticism for increasing taxes.
V: receive, come in for ...
A: heavy, severe, fierce ...
G: ... criticism for raising taxes
     ... criticism for its plan (to build ...)
     ... criticism over the decision (to spend ...)
F: ... come under heavy criticism for not providing ...
     The same criticism has been levelled at ...

2.11 Summary

The growing awareness of the rich contextual relationships in spoken and written discourse means that collocation and word grammar need to become established categories of description for both the teaching and learning of languages. A greater focus needs to be placed on developing the independent language learning skills that will help students develop their proficiency in these areas. In particular, training needs to be given in the constructive use of dictionaries and the vast and varied sources of English that modern technology has made available. Finally, guidance in managing this learning through frameworks such as lexical notebooks needs to be provided.

It is probably true that the role of the language teacher today is moving more and more towards that of learning manager, and as such, a primary aim of teaching must be to raise the students' awareness of their increasing responsibility for, and power over, their own learning.

Discussion Questions

Do you have learners who would use computer-based corpora and concordancing software with confidence?

Do you think it is useful to give all your students this confidence? If not, in what ways can you provide them with similar information?

What sort of information do you encourage your students to record in their vocabulary notebooks?

References:

Brown, P. R. (1994) Lexical Collocation: a strategy for advanced learners, in Modern English Teacher, Vol. 3, No. 2
Lewis, M. (1997) Implementing the Lexical Approach, LTP
Hill, J. and Lewis, M. Eds. (1997) LTP Dictionary of Selected Collocations, LTP
Crowther, J. Ed. (1997) Oxford Advanced Learners Dictionary, Oxford University Press
Swan, M (1996) Language teaching is teaching language, Plenary IATEFL
Concordance data generated by MicroConcord, OUP
[Contact Oxford University Press for details of Wordsmith, referred to on p 42.]

Chapter 3

Revising priorities: from grammatical failure to collocational success

Jimmie Hill

In this chapter, Jimmie Hill suggests that putting lexis rather than grammar at the centre of language teaching is more than just a modest change, it is a revolution. He stresses the size of the mental lexicon needed by even an intermediate learner, and suggests that this means greatly increasing the amount of language input provided in language courses. He draws attention to the sheer number of collocations to be found in texts, and emphasises the need for the teacher to choose the right kinds of text for their learners, then to guide learners so that they can become independent collectors of collocations from input which they meet outside the classroom. Controversially, he suggests that over-emphasising grammar is a major factor in preventing learners from moving on from the intermediate plateau.

3.1 Language and lexis

Devotion to a structural syllabus has dominated ELT for too long, with the study and practice of grammar seen as synonymous with the teaching of accuracy. We are at present in one of those awkward stages in the development of ELT methodology when teachers are still putting into practice ideas which most theoreticians have long abandoned. All manner of ideas are still associated with the obsession with grammar: standards, traditional ways of doing things, how textbooks are written, how tests are constructed, and most inhibitingly of all, perhaps, the expectations both teachers and students bring to textbooks and courses.

When I first started teaching English, we were encouraged to think of grammar as the bones of the language, and vocabulary as the flesh to be added. We now know that language consists largely of prefabricated chunks of lexis. That 'skeleton' image has been consigned proverbially to the cupboard. A central feature of lexis is collocation, an idea that for the first 15 years of my career in ELT I hardly gave a moment's thought to, but which for the past 10 years, has come to play a more and more central part in my thinking about English, the classroom, materials, and methodology. I am not alone. The work of John Sinclair, Dave Willis, Ron Carter, Michael McCarthy, Michael Lewis, and many others, has all contributed to the way teachers today think about lexis and what it means for their teaching.

The more we have become aware of language as a predominantly lexical phenomenon, the more we know that many of our previously cherished structuralist ideas are false. This is one of the most exciting turnarounds in our thinking for a very long time. In one sense, it is a recognition of ways of thinking which we all knew, but which many teachers have denied.

3.2 Language and learning

All language teachers know that the way they teach, and expect their students to learn a second language, is very different from the way they learned their L1. We acquire our L1 efficiently without any explicit knowledge of grammar rules, parts of speech, or knowing what collocation is. During our L1 acquisition we are happy with the idea of making 'mistakes'. We wait for the natural process of acquisition to take its course. We know that our children learn huge chunks of lexis, expressions, idioms, proverbs, nursery rhymes, songs, poems, bedtime stories without necessarily understanding each word. We now realise that in learning such chunks they are also acquiring the pronunciation, stress, and intonation patterns which will remain with them throughout their lives. They are also learning the grammatical system of the L1. No young native speaker of English exposed to *Jack and Jill went up the hill to fetch a pail of water* is aware of concepts such as simple past tense and irregular verbs. And for many children the illustrated 'pail' in the nursery rhyme book will be the closest they ever get to one in their lives, as metal pails have now been largely replaced by plastic buckets. A lexical approach to language and to learning does not break everything down into individual words and structures, but sees language in larger units. It could be seen as a sensible return to traditional ways of learning after a rather futile trip down the dead-end road of structuralism.

It is true that learning an L2 is not the same as learning your L1, but it is also true that the human activity closest in nature to L2 learning is L1 learning. To deny the many similarities seems perverse. It seems sensible to take on board what lessons we can from the lexical nature of language and the lexical ways in which natives learn their mother tongue. In particular, that huge area of language commonly referred to as idiomatic usage, is clearly learned lexically. One of the most important areas of idiomatic language is collocation.

3.3 What is collocation?

Many years ago, J.R. Firth defined collocation as 'the company words keep' – their relationships with other words. Another definition might be 'the way words combine in predictable ways'. When we think of the number of words in English, the number of potential combinations runs into many millions. So, the first and most important fact about the nature of collocation is the sheer number of individual collocations which exist in English. Past assessments of the number of individual words known by an educated native speaker pale into insignificance when compared with the total number of items – words, expressions, idioms, and collocations – which exist in the mental lexicon of the typical educated native speaker. This fact of the size of the mental lexicon must dominate all our methodological thinking. When we believed that grammar was the basis of all language learning, it was quite comforting to know that we had discovered all the English tenses and they could be summarised on half a dozen pages of a grammar book. Grammar – in its assumed finiteness – was a superficially attractive basis for our syllabus. The complete lexicon of English, on the other hand, is enormous. The mental lexicon of any individual is huge, consisting as it does of a vast repertoire of learned phrases of varying degrees of fixedness. Within the mental lexicon, collocation is the most powerful force in the creation and comprehension of all naturally-occurring text.

For teachers who are familiar with the huge impact of corpus linguistics, these observations are obvious, but it is important to remember that for many teachers worldwide the **word** is still the basic unit of language. Corpus linguistics has, however, taught us the importance of looking at natural language in large enough quantities to see recurring patterns of lexis in texts of all kinds. You might like to re-read this article so far and underline all the groups of words which occur in predictable combinations. For example, *encouraged to think, a central feature, for the first X years of my career, a moment's thought, has come to play a more and more central part in my thinking, huge impact,* etc.

3.4 Collocational competence

Even if the word 'collocation' is new to students and to some teachers, the problem of collocational errors is as old as language learning itself. How often do students ask *Can you say X?* – to which the teacher replies: *Well, you can, but we just don't.* If we can say both *It's nice to get out into the open air* and *It's nice to get out in the fresh air,* why can't we say *I need a breath of open air?* And if we can say *an open-air restaurant,* why not then *a fresh-air restaurant?* We have all smiled at the tourist menu which offers *cow tail soup* or the student who talked about *silly cow disease.* We are familiar with the concept of communicative competence, but we need to add the concept of **collocational competence** to our thinking.

Any analysis of students' speech or writing shows a lack of this collocational competence. Lack of competence in this area forces students into grammatical mistakes because they create longer utterances because they do not know the collocations which express precisely what they want to say. Teachers often then focus on correcting the grammar mistakes, failing to realise that it will make no difference – the mistakes are not made because of faulty grammar but a lack of collocations. For example, a student could easily invent the cumbersome *His disability will continue until he dies* because (s)he lacks the *verb + adjective + noun* collocation *He has a permanent disability.* Even if learners successfully navigate the grammar, what they produce often sounds awkward and very 'intermediate'. Analysis of students' essay writing often shows a serious lack of collocational competence with 'de-lexicalised' verbs such as *get, put, make, do, bring, take.* For example, *I make exercise every morning in the gym.* Students with good ideas often lose marks because they do not know the four or five most important collocates of a key word that is central to what they are writing about. In this respect, collocation is an old problem. Only now, however, are we beginning to see it might be a new solution to many of our learners' problems.

3.5 Collocations, idioms and phrasal verbs

Even during the height of structuralism, we knew that the lexicon was complicated. Apart from individual words, we were keenly aware that multi-word expressions were important. We identified phrasal verbs and idioms as two important areas for students. The rest we labelled 'idiomatic usage'. It is only recently through the rise of corpus linguistics that the extent of the fixedness of much language has been more widely recognised. We know that fixed expressions range from the totally fixed *(An apple a day keeps the doctor away),* through the semi-fixed *(What I'm saying/suggesting/proposing is . . .),* to the fairly loose yet still predictable *(go on holiday).* In one sense all collocation is idiomatic and all idioms and phrasal verbs are collocations – predictable combinations of different kinds. So, how can we use these terms most usefully?

It seems sensible to continue using those terms and categories which language teachers have found useful in the past – idioms and phrasal verbs – while introducing the term *collocation* to name and categorise that language which has previously been ignored or undervalued. Let us look more closely at each of these three categories.

1. Idioms

An idiom is an expression which is relatively fixed and allows little or no change. It is often metaphorical: *He put the cat among the pigeons; Don't count your chickens.* Not all idioms are as pictorial as these two examples. We could think of *catch the bus* or *fired with enthusiasm* as idioms because of the inherently metaphorical use of *catch* and *fire.* The native speaker has no problem with the idea that both *fish* and *buses* can be *caught* or that non-physical things can be *on fire.* If the same verbs are not used in the learners' L1, it is probable that they will have a problem with the English idiomatic use. We need to broaden our concept of idiom to include much more metaphorical usage, which is frequently hardly even recognised as idiomatic by native speakers.

2. Phrasal verbs

Phrasal verbs contain a verb plus one or more particles: *make up* a story, *put the light out*. The meaning may or may not be obvious from the individual words. Again, learners may have no trouble with the literal *put the cat out* but cannot relate that to *put the light out*. Some teachers consider *get on* (in *get on the bus*) as a phrasal verb. Others think of it as verb plus preposition. The distinction is not helpful for the classroom where the emphasis is on **the phrase as a whole** rather than any analysis of it. Arguments aside, the category of phrasal verb is a useful one for both teachers and learners to identify certain items which they are trying to teach and learn.

3. Collocations

As mentioned above, in a sense, all collocations are idiomatic and all phrasal verbs and idioms are collocations or contain collocations, but rather than spending all our time describing and sorting expressions, the real issue for the methodologist is to try to help teachers to make simple categories which will help their students see some order and organisation in the lexicon. ELT has always recognised two types of multi-word item where the patterns have been clear – idioms and phrasal verbs. It is time to introduce our students to one more category of language as it really is – collocation.

A collocation is a predictable combination of words: *get lost, make up for lost time, speak your mind*. Some combinations may be very highly predictable from one of the component words – *foot the bill, mineral water, spring to mind*. Some 'strong' collocations have the status of idioms – *shrug your shoulders* – they are not guessable and are non-generative. Some may be so common that they hardly seem worth remarking upon – *a big flat, a nice car, have lunch*. (As just mentioned, however, native speakers must be careful, because an item which seems unremarkable to them might be a problem to a learner. Because of their L1, some learners may find *eat lunch* or *take lunch* a more obvious choice than *have lunch*.)

Teachers will find it useful to draw their learners' attention to collocations of different kinds. I suggest that the following, in particular, will be of interest:

adjective + noun	*a huge profit*
noun + noun	*a pocket calculator*
verb + adjective + noun	*learn a foreign language*
verb + adverb	*live dangerously*
adverb + verb	*half understand*
adverb + adjective	*completely soaked*
verb + preposition + noun	*speak through an interpreter*

Collocations can, in fact, be much longer. For example: adverb + verb + article + adjective + noun + preposition + noun = *seriously affect the political situation in Bosnia*. The term 'collocation' should help bring **all** these chunks of language to students' attention **as single choices.**

3.6 Collocations and grammar

It is always an oversimplification to divide language up into categories when all the elements of natural language use are interdependent. So, idioms have a grammar and can be minimally variable to fit the speaker's purpose:

Don't	
He	
She's just	*let the cat out of the bag.*
If only you hadn't	
Why did you	

Collocations, too, cannot be divorced from the grammatical context in which they occur. There are two important pedagogical considerations here.

Firstly, it is important that teachers are aware of this. The simple collocation *brush your teeth* is for native speakers predominantly used in the dentist's surgery and in the home when speaking to children or other family members. One of the most common structures in which it will occur is *Have you brushed your teeth yet?* – a parent teaching a child habits of personal hygiene usually at bedtime. One can imagine a husband saying to his wife: *I'll be with you in a minute. I'm just going to brush my teeth.* I imagine few husbands would ask their wives the question that they would ask their young children. We can speculate that sentences such as the following will be rarer than the present perfect and *going to* uses above:

I brushed my teeth . . .
I'm brushing my teeth . . .
I'd brushed my teeth . . .

Secondly, when the child hears the parent asking *Have you brushed your teeth?* something else is going on. The child is hearing the present perfect in a natural context. For perhaps ten years of childhood a parent may ask the question. Children may never use the question themselves until they are parents themselves. What the children have been exposed to is an archetypical example of the present perfect without knowing anything explicit about English tense names. It is clear that the acquisition of generalisable grammar rules must be partly related to the acquisition of lexical chunks containing the grammar in question. Perhaps the inability of our students to acquire some important grammatical areas is based on the implausibility of many of the examples to which we expose them in current EFL grammar books and textbooks [See also pp 163-167]. When we know that native speakers learn language in lexical chunks, it is not unreasonable to assume that learning certain chunks containing these structures will help learners in their acquisition of English grammar patterns as well. [This is another plea to teachers to encourage learners to notice and record language in a linguistic environment in which it naturally occurs. Ed.]

3.7 Why is collocation important?

Collocation is important from a pedagogical point of view for many reasons. I suggest at least these nine are important for teachers:

1. The lexicon is not arbitrary

The first and most obvious reason why collocation is important is because the way words combine in collocations is fundamental to all language use. The lexicon is not arbitrary. We do not speak or write as if language were one huge substitution table with vocabulary items merely filling slots in grammatical structures. To an important extent vocabulary choice is predictable. When a speaker thinks of drinking, he may use a common verb such as *have*. The listener's expectations predict a large number of possibilities: *tea, coffee, milk, mineral water, orange juice*, even *tequila sunrise*, but there would be no expectations of *engine oil, shampoo, sulphuric acid*. The latter liquids are drunk by accident, but linguistically they are not 'probable' in the way that the former are. Looking at a rarer verb – *enhance* – the choice of objects is limited to a relatively small number of nouns or noun patterns, eg *his reputation, the standing of the company*. If the verb is *do*, the choice is far greater, but still limited, eg *his best, the honourable thing*, but not *a mistake*. So, the very definition of collocation – the way words combine – gives it a status which we cannot deny.

2. Predictability

The very predictability of the collocation examples in the previous paragraph gives us another clue as to why collocation is an important pedagogical issue. The present simple is important in classrooms because we can predict its use to an extent which helps learners. In a similar way, there are patterns to collocations which can make learning easier. There are parts of the lexicon which are organised and patterned, and classrooms are, by definition, places where learning is encouraged by using the most efficient means known to teachers and where learners need to be encouraged to notice predictable patterning.

3. The size of the phrasal mental lexicon

Collocation is important because this area of predictability is, as we have seen, **enormous**. Two, three, four and even five-word collocations make up a huge percentage of all naturally-occurring text, spoken or written. Estimates vary, but it is possible that up to 70% of everything we say, hear, read, or write is to be found in some form of fixed expression.

4. The role of memory

We know collocations because we have met them. We then retrieve them from our mental lexicon just as we pull a telephone number or address from our memory.

ELT has not given sufficient thought to this idea. Linguists now give a much greater importance to memorised, familiar, and idiomatic language. There was a reaction against these ideas during the sixties and seventies when methodologists reacted against any suggestion that learning by heart had any place in L2 learning. Phrase-books, which had played an important part in language learning for centuries, were scorned in favour of the all-powerful grammatical model of language learning.

Every native speaker parent knows how children love to hear the same rhymes and stories night after night to the extent that they can say the rhymes and tell the stories themselves. As adults we all have a huge store of memorised text in our heads, ranging from poetry, addresses, telephone numbers, proverbs, idioms, sayings, clichés, to catchphrases, advertising slogans and jokes. Most often we have made no attempt to learn these items; knowing them is simply part of what we mean by being a native speaker. How do I know *lead on Macduff, coughs and sneezes spread diseases, flavour of the month, free gratis and for nothing, each and every one of us, Don't forget the fruit gums Mum,* and even *That's the way the cookie crumbles?* I may never use them. Indeed, I may be allergic to anyone who does use them! The fact of the matter (itself a good example of a fixed phrase) is that every native speaker has a vast store of these obviously fixed expressions. We have a much **bigger** store of collocations, ready for use when required.

As language teachers, it is obvious that we have underestimated the role of memory in language learning. Not enough research is available to us at present to make useful statements about how memory can be influenced. We do know, however, that the most crucial element in a learner's acquisition of a lexical item is the number of times it is heard or read in a context where it is at least partially understood. We also know it is more important to **hear** or **read** an item than to use it. Communicative methodology mistakenly assumed that early production was all important. What is obvious is that what the language learners are **exposed to** from the earliest stages is crucial. Good quality input should lead to good quality retrieval. Impoverished input will lead to impoverished retrieval.

5. Fluency

Collocation allows us to think more quickly and communicate more efficiently. Native speakers can only speak at the speed they do because they are calling on a vast repertoire of ready-made language, immediately available from their mental lexicons. Similarly, they can listen at the speed of speech and read quickly because they are constantly recognising multi-word units rather than processing everything word-by-word. One of the main reasons the learner finds listening or reading difficult is not because of the density of new words, but the **density of unrecognised collocations**. The main difference between native and non-native speakers is that the former have met far more English and so can recognise and produce these 'ready-made chunks', which enable them to **process** and **produce** language at a much faster rate.

6. Complex ideas are often expressed lexically

Typical intermediate student speech, for example, is laboured, one word at a time, and uses simple vocabulary to express both simple and complicated ideas. This inevitably causes problems. Simple language is ideal for the expression of simple ideas. Complex ideas are difficult to express in complex language; they are even **more** difficult to express in simple language. But the complexity needed here is not convoluted grammar; it is usually lexical – complex noun phrases, frequently made of supposedly 'easy' words. The more exposure students have to good quality input and the more awareness they develop of the lexical nature of language, the more they will recognise and eventually produce longer chunks themselves.

The traditional Present–Practise–Produce paradigm, for so long the accepted orthodoxy, tends to over-emphasise the 'practise' stage, when in reality the 'present' and 'produce' stages are the most important. This does not mean that practice is unimportant. While it is true that you do not 'learn' new language by speaking, it is only by speaking that you can develop confidence. However, we need to place a much greater emphasis on good-quality written and spoken input at lower and intermediate levels than is currently the case.

7. Collocation makes thinking easier

Paradoxically, the reason we can think new things and speak at the speed of thought is because we are **not** using new language all the time. Collocation allows us to name complex ideas quickly so that we can continue to manipulate the ideas without using all our brainspace to focus on the form of words. Try to say *manipulate ideas* or *brainspace* more efficiently! Both are recognised *verb + noun* and *noun + noun* collocations. It is a safe conclusion that collocation is an important key to fluency. It is one of the sacred cows of EFL methodology that fluency comes with practice. Any teacher who has worked in Scandinavia or Holland, where English is widely spoken, knows this to be false. Advanced students do not become more fluent by being given lots of opportunities to be fluent. They become more fluent when they acquire more chunks of language for instant retrieval. As Stephen Krashen has pointed out, acquisition crucially depends on the quantity and quality of input.

8. Pronunciation is integral

I will always remember a lecture at TESOL France some years ago when Michael Swan asked me to read a poem to his audience in Scots – a language similar in structure to English, but with enough significant differences in vocabulary to make it only partially comprehensible. Because I was able to read the poem meaningfully, ie chunking it correctly, the audience all laughed in the correct places. In one sense they 'understood' the poem while not understanding a large proportion of the individual words. Most teachers will have had the experience of watching and enjoying a Shakespeare play. Few will understand fully the nuances of Shakespeare's language. The actors, however, speak the lines meaningfully, correctly chunked for us.

Because learners create much of what they say from **individual** words, their pronunciation, stress, and intonation, can be difficult for the listener. The great added bonus to knowing a large number of collocations and other longer expressions is that if learners learn the stress pattern of a phrase **as a whole**, their stress and intonation will be better.

9. Recognising chunks is essential for acquisition

There are immediate methodological implications. Teachers should read texts aloud in class so that students hear the text correctly chunked. In class we should do **no** unseen reading aloud and less silent reading. The reason students find unseen reading so difficult is because they don't recognise the chunks – they read every word as if it were separate from every other word, so during silent reading students may be chunking totally wrongly. And mis-chunking matters. Correctly understood and stored, lexical items should be available for immediate use. Students cannot store items correctly in their mental lexicon if they have not identified them correctly; incorrectly chunked, the input will either not be stored at all or will be wrongly stored. In either case it cannot be available for retrieval and use – put simply, students cannot learn from input which they mis-chunk.

3.8 Collocation in texts

It is interesting to examine written texts from different genres from a collocational point of view. It soon emerges that collocation is an important feature of all such texts, although different kinds of texts do exhibit different collocational characteristics, making some texts more suitable than others for the EFL classroom. Let us compare fiction, a financial report, a newspaper article and finally, a typical EFL text. Collocations which are of interest are underlined.

1. George Eliot's *Middlemarch*

The following short extract shows that collocation is nothing new, but is important even in a literary text considered a classic:

> Overworked Mrs Dagley – a thin, worn woman, from whose life pleasure had so entirely vanished that she had not even any <u>Sunday clothes</u> which could give her satisfaction in <u>preparing for church</u> – had already <u>had a misunderstanding</u> with her husband since he had <u>come home</u>, and was <u>in low spirits</u>, <u>expecting the worst</u>.

The temptation is to think that 'good writers' do not use such 'ready-made, off-the-shelf' tricks such as collocation, but they do.

There are arguments for more collocations in this extract, but most readers would agree with those underlined. A novelist, by definition, is free to make their own word combinations – in other words, to break our expectations. And it is in the breaking of the conventional that the greatness of great literature partly resides. So, to describe Mrs Dagley as a 'worn woman' evokes her physical and mental state, but could not be guessed. The phrase is Eliot's very own.

2. Frank McCourt's *Angela's Ashes*

> The new rich people go home after Mass on Sundays all airs and stuff themselves with meat and potatoes, sweets and cakes galore, and they think nothing of drinking their tea from delicate little cups which stand in saucers to catch the tea that overflows.

Here a modern novelist uses six identifiable collocations in the space of a few lines of text. While writing something original and creative both Eliot and McCourt rely on their store of ready-for-use expressions. My previous argument that we use collocations in speech to give us thinking time does not hold here since the writer has lots of time to think of new and original ways of expression. The fact that Eliot and McCourt use collocations so readily suggests that the other reason they are common is because they **express precisely what we wish to express** with or without time constraints.

3. Financial report

> Shares in Independent Insurance recovered by more than 5 per cent yesterday after the company bucked the trend in the insurance market by reporting a 22 per cent increase in underwriting profit. The shares, which fell sharply last year after the company spoke of difficult trading rose 14p to 263.5p.

Financial English is dominated by a number of predictable collocations, several of which are used in this short extract: *shares recovered, shares fell sharply, shares rose, buck the trend, the insurance market, difficult trading.*

Any course in Financial English would need to identify some of the common collocational patterns, verbs which combine with *share,* while also preparing learners for the large number of metaphorical expressions such as *buck the trend* which are common in such texts.

4. Newspaper article

> The world of bullfighting has discovered a new legend in the form of a baby-faced 16-year-old called Julian Lopez, but known as "El Juli", who has become the youngest fully-fledged matador ever.
>
> El Juli, a shy and introverted teenager, has been booked up for the

big bullfighting tournaments of the forthcoming season and is expected to kill more than 200 bulls in his first full season in Spain.

The teenager has spent most of his time in Latin America since he qualified as a matador last October when he was still just 15.

His skill and courage has seen him awarded the ultimate accolade in bullfighting – being carried out of the bullring on the fans' shoulders – in more than a dozen Latin American cities in recent weeks.

Quite a lot of this language is worthy of comment. Notice these patterns:

a) *the world of* sport/art/opera/ballroom dancing etc.
b) he re-appeared *in the form of* a creature half-human, half-bird.
c) *the (superlative adjective) . . . ever*: the youngest fully-fledged matador ever, the best holiday ever, the most expensive motorbike ever.
d) There seem to be two collocations combined in: *A baby-faced 16-year-old called,* namely *a baby-faced 16-year-old* and *a 16-year-old called . . .*
e) Finally, *awarded the ultimate accolade* is a very strong collocation typical of such newspaper texts.

The first and most obvious point to make about factual texts like this is the high percentage of words which occur in fixed phrases and collocations. This is completely typical of such texts. Collocation is either so commonplace that it is unremarkable or so inherent in text that it should have a central place in all teaching. These texts are clearly more suited to the EFL classroom than the extracts taken from fiction.

Looking at the bullfighting text from a teaching point of view, it would be madness to try to bring **all** the collocations to the attention of students. We choose texts for class use for different reasons: because we think students will be interested in the topic; because there is language which might be immediately useful; because the language is of a quality to which students should be exposed. Over-exploitation of any one aspect will kill students' interest. Class time should be spent on a few useful collocations. Students should then be encouraged to study the rest themselves at home.

A collocation will be worth drawing to students' attention if it satisfies two conditions – it is suitable for their level **and** it has some common currency, such as the phrase *qualify as a . . .* .The 'level' of an item will always be a subjective issue, but I suggest the following rough divisions from the text above:

Elementary:	*spend time, still just 15, in recent weeks*
Intermediate:	*the world of . . . , known as . . . , the youngest . . . ever, qualify as a . . .*
Advanced:	*a shy and introverted teenager, the forthcoming season, awarded the ultimate accolade.*

The remaining collocations fall into the most important teaching category – those which are not worth spending class time on unless students ask about them. In a structuralist approach teachers did not comment on every grammatical point in a text; so in a lexical approach it would be misguided to 'milk' every text for the last drop of lexis.

5. EFL coursebook texts

In some ways, the most interesting texts to consider are those chosen for inclusion in popular EFL coursebooks – texts of the type teachers are used to dealing with every day in class. Examining a single two-hundred-word extract from the popular *Headway* series (*Upper Intermediate* p 77) it was easy to identify at least the following collocations which teachers could usefully draw to learners' attention:

plan a family	*my best friend*
have a problem	*have the same sense of humour*
share interests	*completely obsessed with*
a lovely age for (a child)	*grow up suddenly*
went to school	*grow away from (your family)*
a teenage daughter/son	*an endless stream of (people)*
I told her off	*in front of (my) friends*

And the following are arguably just as useful:

have the one child	*by the time I'd*
it might have been nice to . . .	*we were closest*
have a son	*they'd gone away*
I see her as . . .	*for days afterwards*

This means over twenty useful collocations – including some relatively long ones containing important grammatical features as part of the lexical item – in a text of only 200 words. The conclusion one must come to is that well-chosen coursebook texts are full of collocational expressions. For students to get the most out of such texts, their attention has to be drawn to that wealth and density of collocation.

There are immediate classroom implications for how we deal with texts. We should be asking students to **predict** collocations which are in the text by identifying and gapping them. We should be asking students to **notice** and **underline** useful ones, and encouraging them to **store** them in their notebooks in some retrievable way, along with the L1 equivalent of **the whole collocation**. Making sense of text involves not only understanding new words; it is intimately bound up with the ability to identify collocations.

3.9 Teaching collocation

In order to teach collocation we have to give it the same kind of status in our methodology as other aspects of language such as pronunciation, intonation, stress, and grammar. We have to see it as being as central to language acquisition as those other aspects of language which we have long recognised. 50 years ago nobody in the medical world had heard of DNA. Today it is central to much medical research. The same is true of lexis in general and collocation in particular. Collocation is not an added bonus which we pay attention to once students have become sufficiently advanced. Collocation should play an important part in our teaching from lesson one.

1. Teaching individual collocations

In the same way that we teach individual words – vocabulary – we need to teach collocations. Rather than wait for students to meet common collocations for themselves, we need to present them in context just as we would present individual words. Here are some examples: *have a bath, make friends, fall in love.*

At a higher level, when students are learning less common vocabulary, we must be aware that some words are used in a very restricted number of collocations. There is no point in knowing the meaning of the words *impetuous* or *initiative* unless you also know the collocations: *impetuous behaviour, take the initiative.*

When teaching a new word, teach some of its most common collocations at the same time. If the word is *ferry*, teach:

> *go on the car ferry*
> *a roll-on roll-off ferry*
> *take the ferry from (Liverpool) to (Belfast).*

If the word is *belief* teach: *strong beliefs, have a belief, belief in God / the power of medicine / yourself.* But you might want to choose which class you teach *beggar belief* to – even if it is one of the 'strongest' collocations of *belief*. Strong collocations tend to be rare, and we do not want to replace teaching obscure words with teaching obscure collocations. A good rule, however, is never to teach a new word – particularly a noun – without giving a few common collocates.

This idea that knowing the meaning of a word is useless unless you also know something of how the word is used is relatively new in ELT. Until very recently, dictionaries were seen only as decoding devices, designed to help students understand the meaning of words they were not sure of. They were not seen as encoding or 'productive' – helping students to compose their own text. It is probably asking too much of any one dictionary that it does both. It is definitely worth emphasising to students that they do not really 'know' or 'own' a word unless they also know **how that word is used**, which means knowing something about its collocational field. There are many pairs or groups of words such as *date/appointment/meeting* or *broad/wide* where the difference between the words is only clear from a knowledge of their different collocational fields.

TASK

Which of the verbs *speak, say, tell* fit best into the gaps in these authentic examples?

1. I can't . . . for the rest of the staff, though.

2. As I . . . , they've already appointed somebody.

3. You'd better do exactly what the doctor . . . .

4. Don't worry. Everything you . . . me is confidential.

5. These figures don't . . . us what will happen next month.

6. It's too soon to . . . whether an agreement can be reached.

7. UN sources . . . the agreement goes much further than any previous one.

8. To . . . you the truth, I was half expecting it.

9. It may be that actions will . . . louder than words.

10. Can I . . . to Mr Harrison, please?

11. Shall we . . . two o'clock?

12. . . . me about it!

These examples – and they are only a small selection of these three verbs – clearly show that it is not possible to give a simple explanation of the difference of meaning with words of this kind.

2. Making students aware of collocation

As mentioned above, the most significant feature of collocation is the sheer number of individual collocations needed for a mature adult lexicon. With limited class time teachers can only teach some of the most common. If, as methodologists tell us, we should teach no more than 10 new words per lesson, given that half might be learned, a normal school year of lessons will only add 500 words to a student's vocabulary. This strongly suggests vocabulary learning **techniques** are more important than the teaching of individual words. The same is true for idioms, fixed expressions and collocations.

What teachers must do is make students aware of collocation as a vital key to language learning. On the simplest level, teachers could encourage students to think bigger than the word – always to look for the two- or three-word expression. Noticing is an important stage in learning. Asking students to underline all *verb + noun* collocations in a text will be a typical exercise. Taking a common word and asking students to find as many collocates as they can will be another typical activity in awareness-raising. As we saw above, with a common verb like *speak* we cannot say that students really know the word unless they know at least the following possibilities:

speak a foreign language	*speak (French)*	*speak fluently*
speak your mind	*speak clearly*	*speak with a (Welsh) accent*
speak in public	*speak openly*	*speak volumes*

Such a verb would have received scant attention in the past and such attention as it did receive would be likely to concentrate on 'explaining' the difference between *speak, talk* and *tell*. As we saw in the task above, however, exploring the collocational field is far more helpful than any explanation of the supposed differences.

3. Extending what students already know

Extend students' collocational competence with words they already know as well as teaching new words. A student with a vocabulary of 2,000 words will only be able to function in a fairly limited way. A different student with 2,000 words, but **collocationally competent** with those words, will also be far more **communicatively competent**. Many native speakers function perfectly well using a limited vocabulary with which they are collocationally competent.

The message for ELT is that more class time needs to be spent with some of the more common words, in particular the 'de-lexicalised' verbs, *get, put, take, do, make* etc. Students who know 2,000 words and six collocations with each, know 12,000 expressions. For example:

make: *make a mistake / a meal / trouble / a complaint / friends / space for*
end: *at the end of / in the end / come to an end / to the bitter end / at a loose end / at the end of the day*
at: *at once / at first / at work / at school / at college / not at all*

As the last example shows, the words with **least** content are closest to traditional grammar. The discriminating exploration of word-grammar is more likely to help learners than either the more exotic parts of traditional grammar or teaching 'difficult' words.

4. Storing collocations

An organised lexical notebook is essential for all students. Deciding where to put an item, writing it down, and looking at it again along with other similar items is all part of the constant revisiting of language which is part of the learning process. Students' lexical notebooks do not need to be glossy professionally-produced products. The simplest looseleaf binder with blank pages can be turned into an organised lexicon very easily. We need to manage students' notebooks in the same way we manage other areas of their learning.

It is easy to imagine a collocation section arranged in the following ways:

1. Grammatically: sections such as *noun + noun, adjective + noun, verb + noun, adverb + adjective*
2. By common key word: collocations with *do, make, get, up, speak* etc.
3. By topic: collocations to talk about holidays, travel, work etc.

We do not know how we store language in our mental lexicons. We do know that we store it in patterns of different kinds which allow us to retrieve it instantly. Storing lexis in an organised way in a notebook so that it can be revised and retrieved quickly must be better than not storing it, or simply listing new items without organising them. One of the advantages of this is that this makes learning less 'materials-dependent'. In resource-poor countries most students often have access to a simple notebook when glossy UK-produced coursebooks are financially beyond them.

3.10 Choosing which collocations to teach

Just as important as choosing which collocations to teach is deciding what **not** to teach. Avoid the temptation to teach every collocation which comes up in class. If collocation is an idea you may not have been very conscious of in your past teaching, it is very easy to go overboard. They are everywhere. Texts of all kinds are packed with them. Draw students' attention to important ones and let them find and record others for themselves. Do not, however, confuse rare and obscure collocations with important ones. Choosing which collocations to teach and which ones to ignore, given limited classroom time, involves understanding **collocational strength**. As we shall see, the most important for the classroom are what we may call medium-strength collocations.

1. Unique collocations

It is useful to think of collocations on a cline or spectrum from those which are probably unique/fixed/strong to those which are flexible/weak. Several commentators have pointed out the uniqueness of *foot* used as a verb in the collocation *foot the bill*. We cannot imagine *footing the invoice*, or *footing the coffee*. Similarly, we *shrug our shoulders*, but no other part of our anatomy.

2. Strong collocations

A large number of collocations, although not unique, are strong or very strong. Predictably, we may talk of *trenchant criticism* or *rancid butter,* although this does not mean that other things cannot be *trenchant* or *rancid*. We often have *ulterior motives* or *harbour grudges* while being *reduced* or even *moved to tears*. Such strong collocations are not unique, but it is clear that any knowledge of the words *trenchant, rancid, motive, grudge,* or *tears* would be seriously incomplete without some knowledge of these strong collocates.

3. Weak collocations

Many things can be *long* or *short, cheap* or *expensive, good* or *bad*. Students can make combinations such as *blue shirt, red car* etc; they can apply the colours in English in a similar way to their own language. In fact, the picture is not as simple as that, but for most teaching purposes we pretend that it is.

However, there is something 'more predictable', and so more collocational, about these examples: *a white shirt, white wine, red wine, red hair, a black mood, a blue film.*

Similarly, most teachers would agree that the adjective *good* is not very interesting from a teaching point of view. It can be applied to anything – a meal, a journey, a government. But notice what happens with some slightly larger multi-word expressions containing *good*:

> *It'll take you a good hour.*
> *Oh, he's a good age.*
> *He'll do it in his own good time.*

We need to recognise that easy words have many uses; they are part of many weak collocations, but may also be a component of many fixed or semi-fixed expressions. Students need to be made aware of their more predictable collocations.

4. Medium-strength collocations

The main learning load for all language users is not at the strong or weak ends of the collocational spectrum, but in the middle – those many thousands of collocations which make up a large part of what we say and write. Most intermediate students will know the words *hold* and *conversation*, but may not know that you can *hold a conversation*. They know the words *make* and *mistake*, but have not stored *make a mistake* in their mental lexicons **as a single item**. [Remember the key point about lexical items is precisely that they represent single choices of meaning, and are recognised and stored as single items. Ed.]

This, then, explains why learners with even 'good vocabularies' still have problems. They may know a lot of words, but their collocational competence with those words is very limited. I have come to the view that the main thrust of classroom vocabulary teaching at intermediate level and above should be to increase students' collocational competence with their basic vocabulary, while stressing to them the need to acquire more new words on their own through independent reading.

A *nomadic tribe* is a strong collocation because *nomadic* collocates with a very limited number of nouns; *a big flat* is a weak collocation and of little interest to teachers, but *He's recovering from a major operation* is a complex medium-strength collocation. Each individual word may be known to students, but they probably do not know the whole collocation. They are more likely to build the idea phrase by phrase: *My father – he's getting better – he had a big operation.* Full marks for communicating meaning, but more of an effort for both speaker and listener. It is this area of **medium-strength collocations** which is of prime importance in expanding learners' mental lexicons.

3.11 Pedagogical implications

Although I meet many teachers who are trying to incorporate lexical ideas into their teaching, it seems that what we now know about the nature of lexis, and collocation in particular, raises important issues for everyone involved in language teaching.

Theories of language and theories of language learning are inextricably linked. In ELT we now have a more comprehensive model of language, one which gives at least equal importance to the lexicon as to the grammar. We also have a more holistic view of how second languages are learned.

In class we may adhere loosely to a Present–Practise–Produce model, but we are also acutely aware of its limitations. We are readier to accept that the best learning probably happens outside the classroom when students are reading, listening, watching and interacting with the language in a book, newspaper, on radio or TV, or with a native speaker. Increasingly, too, many learners interact with the language, with both native and non-native speakers, on the internet. In this environment, recognising and adopting collocation as a major element in our teaching has several important implications:

1. Review the language content of courses

It is clear that lexis should be one of the central organising principles of our syllabus. Unfortunately, in classrooms, grammar still tends to rule, and sentence grammar at that! Greater emphasis on lexis must mean less emphasis on grammar. Accuracy must be treated as a late-acquired skill. Greater emphasis on 'larger chunks' of language also means that grammar and vocabulary merge into one another. The dividing line is much less clear-cut than teachers and textbooks often pretend.

The sheer size of the learning load makes change inevitable. Accepting that the learning load is not 40,000 items but nearer 400,000 (and probably greater) means that the syllabus must be reviewed, and criteria for what to teach agreed, based on four parameters:

a. Frequency of occurrence in spoken and written text. Although very important, frequency alone should not be the over-riding parameter. An item may be highly frequent in one genre, but not in another. Another item may be highly frequent in native-speaker English but may be unsuitable for learners.

b. Suitability for foreign and second language use. This is a subjective, but important parameter. Experienced teachers are aware that some common native-speaker items will sound silly or inappropriate if used by learners. Such items often depend on subtle features of intonation, pronunciation and context. If learners have not mastered these features, they risk being misunderstood, giving offence or at least giving an impression they do not intend.

c. Level: the lexical learning needs of elementary students are very different from those of the advanced student. Different kinds of item and different learning strategies are appropriate at different stages.

d. Type of course: it is clear that items typical in business English or any form of ESP may have little or no place in a general English course, while for general English it may be possible to predict a certain number of basic collocations for some of the commonest words of the language.

2. Increase language input

If languages are to an extent learned lexically, this should be reflected in our methodology. The main implication is that learners need a great deal more input than they received in most traditional language courses. The **quantity**, **type**, and **quality** of input need to be reviewed. One of the major failings of the communicative approach was that one learner's deficient output became another's deficient intake. Modern task-based approaches are in danger of falling into the same trap. While recognising the need for expert direction and monitoring by the teacher, they focus very much on student output, student performance.

Nobody would deny the importance of output, but the main thrust of language teaching must be to create opportunities for students to **acquire more and more language**. This means maximising the amount of appropriate quality input available to the learners. The role of the teacher, the classroom, and materials all need to be changed. Instead of being a language practice facilitator, the teacher should be first and foremost a language **provider** and the expert who helps students notice useful and interesting language. This might even – horror of horrors – mean increased teacher talking time, **providing** the talk is controlled to provide good quality, appropriate input. Language practice, while important, is secondary. The classroom should be a language-rich environment with interesting English on the walls, a library of graded readers, and internet-access if possible. Published materials should contain more natural language with more activities focussed on the language and on individual learning. In short, the emphasis should be on activities and strategies which aid acquisition.

3. Review strategies at different levels

Again, the sheer size of the mental lexicon has implications for vocabulary teaching strategies at all levels. At elementary level the priority is to increase the number of individual words learners know. These are best learned along with a small number of collocates. For example, there is no point in learners knowing the word *holiday* unless they also know that you *go on holiday,* but they will probably be intermediate before they learn *a package/ beach/adventure holiday*. Intermediate students need more new words with more collocates while also increasing their collocational competence with words they already know.

At levels above intermediate, students need to read widely and it is virtually impossible to predict what items a student 'should' learn. By this stage students should be autonomous learners and have understood that learning a new word without some of its collocates is a waste of time, or at least very inefficient. Advanced students will always be adding to their store of collocates even of words they learned as elementary students. For example, all advanced students are familiar with the words *book, family, holiday* and *light* but how many would be familiar with the following collocations:

a coffee-table book	*the nuclear family*
a busman's holiday	*a blinding light*

We also need to develop techniques to help students to record lexis in helpful ways – ways which reveal patterns and which are easily accessible for revision purposes. If teachers spend more time in class at intermediate and advanced levels exploring words and their collocates and recording them systematically, students will become more skilled at doing it for themselves. At present, most students equate vocabulary work with learning 'new', more difficult words. Often this can mean the words are also more obscure and correspondingly of limited use to the learner. The main thrust of vocabulary work in most classes should be to make students more collocationally competent with the words with which they are already partly familiar.

4. Translation

There are clear implications for translation. It should never have been discarded. Many students have to do it. It is essential in much business English and ESP. Lexis is an area where literal translation is often impossible. A collocation in English may be totally different in Spanish or Japanese. The unique skills in this area of the non-native teacher must be recognised.

5. Language model

This raises the issue of what our model should be. English is taught throughout the world, predominantly by non-native speakers, so that their students can communicate mostly with other non-native speakers. Yet collocation is dictated by the native-speaker speech community. Some collocation errors will matter because communication will be impaired, while others are more like surface grammar errors. Teachers should no more correct every collocation mistake than they should correct every grammar mistake. As usual, the communication of meaning and the learner's current intergrammar should be the decisive factors.

3.12 Summary – less grammar, more lexis

It is accepted that recent developments in corpus linguistics have forced us to change our view of language. This means it is time for a re-evaluation of many of our accepted ideas about learning and teaching. Corpus linguistics is going to change the content of what we teach radically. These ideas on collocation are only the first rumblings.

In ELT we have grown accustomed to the idea that language – the content of what we teach – is a rule-governed system and if we could just learn the rules, we would acquire the language. We now know that this idea is so at odds with the way both first, and subsequent, languages are learned that there is no point in hanging on to it as any kind of model for learning. To be efficient, learning must reflect the nature of what it is we are learning. Language is proven to be a mixture of the totally novel, the absolutely fixed, the relatively fixed, and all held together with fairly simple structures which we call grammar. The largest learning load and the one which is never complete – even for native speakers – is mastering the lexicon. Within the lexicon, collocation is one of the biggest definable areas to which all learners need to be introduced from lesson one.

Insistence on accuracy inhibits production and makes students concentrate on language at or below sentence level. Competence depends on being able to decode and take part in discourse, whether spoken or written. Similarly, there is little point in spending a lot of class time presenting individual items of vocabulary, practising them, and trying to set up situations for students to use them. The acquisition of individual items depends not on students' using them 20 times in one lesson, but on meeting them, perhaps 10 times, in different contexts, at different times.

The fact is, language courses are finite – time is limited. If we are to start teaching collocation, we must stop teaching something else to make room. The answer must be to spend less time on formal grammar work, restricted to a small range of traditional EFL 'structures', regularly revisited. A second fact is that most students are intermediate. **Spending a lot of class time on traditional EFL grammar condemns learners to remaining on the intermediate plateau**. Helping learners to become 'advanced' needs a huge injection of lexis. It is lexis in general, and collocational competence in particular, which allows students to read more widely, understand more quickly, and speak more fluently.

By taking a finite list of grammatical structures as their basis, many current coursebooks and ministry syllabuses are seriously flawed. Progress in English for all post-elementary learners depends on sufficient lexical input, of which collocation is the single most important element.

[Parts of this article first appeared in Issue 11 of *English Teaching Professional*.]

Discussion Questions

Different texts contain different kinds of collocations. What kinds of texts do you think will be of most use to your learners? Are there kinds of texts which you think will not be particularly useful? How does your choice compare with the texts you find in coursebooks?

How many items do you think you should present in a single lesson, or on a single day of teaching? How many of those do you expect your learners to really master so that they can use them themselves?

How would you explain the difference between an intermediate and an advanced learner? Is it, as Jimmie Hill suggests, a matter of the size of the learner's mental lexicon?

Do you agree that over-emphasising grammar can actively prevent learners from developing beyond the intermediate plateau?

Chapter 4

Integrating collocation into a reading and writing course

Jane Conzett

Jane Conzett works on a typical Intensive English Program in the United States. She describes how her reading and writing classes have changed as a result of her dissatisfaction with the way she was reacting to errors in her students' written assignments. Like Morgan Lewis, she found that some theoretical reading helped her understand the problem better, and guided her towards teaching strategies that she finds more effective. She emphasises the importance of both context and collocation in presenting new words.

Non-American readers need to be aware that language teaching in the US may vary from what is usual in the British and European tradition. Jane writes from the perspective of an American Intensive English Program, but many of her experiences and conclusions parallel those of George Woolard and Morgan Lewis described earlier.

4.1 Background

As an instructor in an Intensive English Program (IEP) in the United States, my discovery and understanding of collocation actually resulted from my own frustration with vocabulary study in the classroom. Before I describe how this came about, a brief outline of a typical American IEP may be helpful for readers not familiar with such programs. The goal of most IEPs is to improve students' ability to use English for academic and professional purposes, most often in preparation for academic work in American colleges and universities. Term length ranges from 8-16 weeks; class size averages about 12. The approach to curriculum is frequently content-based, and core courses may be integrated so that students enroll in combined skills courses such as reading/writing, or listening/speaking, or they may be taught as single-skill courses.

Many programs offer electives such as pronunciation, computer skills, or TOEFL preparation, the latter because the Test of English as a Foreign Language is the proficiency test most often required by American universities for admission to degree programs. Students are in class an average of 18 to 25 hours per week, and they complete several hours of homework outside of class each day.

My frustration as a teacher came about when, despite careful, contextualized study of vocabulary in my reading and writing classes, my students often used their new vocabulary incorrectly when they moved from receptive to productive language. As I struggled to remedy what wasn't working in my classes, I headed to the library for some help and stumbled almost serendipitously upon the notion of collocation, a word I had previously never heard of. The proverbial light bulb went on. I recognized from a description of collocations that was included as part of Nation's book, *Teaching and Learning Vocabulary*, that this was precisely where I and my students were stumbling. Since that time, I have changed my approach to teaching vocabulary in my reading and writing classes, testing and trying methods that have resulted in more accurate language production by my students.

As my knowledge and understanding of collocation has grown, my overall approach to teaching has changed in some subtle, but important ways as well. In the context of our IEP, a typical one in the United States, I would like to describe how this gradual change came about, and share some practical ways to implement practice and training in collocations within existing curricula.

4.2 The need to build vocabulary

As do many American IEPs today, our program teaches reading and writing as an integrated course. Students read articles or texts, often grouped thematically around a particular content area such as 'work and careers', or 'society and aging', and then respond to the readings in writing, using a variety of discourse types. This approach mimics the typical interaction with the English language that future graduate or undergraduate students will encounter at the university. When these reading and writing tasks are given to non-native speakers, a natural response is for students to bemoan their lack of vocabulary, and we teachers – most of us second language learners at some point in our own lives – can certainly see their point. In fact, L2 learners are at a tremendous disadvantage when one compares their vocabulary to that of native speakers. If we are defining vocabulary as just individual words, Nation and others estimate the size of a native-speaker undergraduate student's active vocabulary (words used in speech and writing) at 20,000 words. Crow estimates a much greater passive vocabulary – 60,000 to 100,000 words – for this same average student, but even the most conservative estimate of native-speaker vocabulary is enough to be discouraging to every ESL student, even those whose language is quite 'advanced'.

How can teachers help their students feel less like Sisyphus pushing his stone up the hill as they study vocabulary? Current approaches reflect a shift in thinking. The communicative approach to language teaching, popular in the US in the 1970s and 1980s, downplayed explicit vocabulary instruction, with the notion that students could learn vocabulary implicitly, guessing and inferring from rich context. Sökmen has described how this approach met with several problems relating to the slowness of the method and the rate of acquisition, the inaccuracy of some of the 'guesses', its disregard for individual abilities and learning styles, and especially, the lack of retention of the new vocabulary.

Recent research, while not advocating total abandonment of inferring from context, which is a valuable reading skill in its own right, supports the notion that some systematic, explicit study of vocabulary is vital to gaining language proficiency. As Sökmen concludes:

> The pendulum has swung from direct teaching of vocabulary (the grammar-translation method) to incidental (the communicative approach) and now, laudably, back to the middle: implicit and explicit learning.

The question today is no longer whether or not to teach vocabulary explicitly, but how to go about it.

4.3 Explicit vocabulary study

Recognizing the importance of explicit vocabulary study, our IEP has in recent years made it an explicit part of the reading and writing curriculum. The means of achieving this vary, depending on the teachers' preferences and the students' proficiency levels. Some teachers choose vocabulary builder books based on word-lists; some choose books based on roots and affixes; others study vocabulary in context in teacher-created lists based on the readings the students do in class. All of these choices have their advantages. With limited time one can see the efficiency of studying high-frequency vocabulary; books based on roots and affixes can help students make educated guesses at the meanings of new words, with the added benefit of helping students who struggle with English spelling patterns. It can, for example, be reassuring to students to know that *medicine* and *medical* have the same root spelling of *medic*, even though one would not be able to guess this from the way the words are pronounced. In-context study of vocabulary encountered in reading has the well-known advantages of point-of-need relevance to the student, and natural, real-life examples of usage.

The vocabulary books I have used have been for the most part well-written, with ample opportunities for students to practice the vocabulary through in-context cloze exercises, matching, fill-in-the-blank, etc. Interestingly, the students have always been enthusiastic about explicit vocabulary study, perhaps because it has the initial appearance of being something reassuringly concrete in the complex world of second language acquisition.

With good books, motivated students, and plenty of practice, I felt destined for success. Instead, even if the students scored well on passive skills exams, when they tried to actually use the new vocabulary, something often went disappointingly wrong.

Here are some sentences that were produced by students in our IEP after they had received explicit vocabulary instruction for the underlined words:

Be careful. That snake is <u>toxic</u>.
We will <u>sever</u> this class because it is too large.
A Ferrari is a very <u>potent</u> car.

My usual response to production errors of this type was to give the student partial or half credit because they had obviously understood the meaning of the words despite the awkward sentences. Sometimes I wrote 'word choice' on their paper, indicating the error type. When a student asked, *But doesn't toxic mean poisonous?* I would give a response along the lines of, *Well, yes, but we don't usually use it that way,* which left both of us feeling frustrated and dissatisfied. I should point out that the student obviously had communicated the intended meaning, and in that regard was successful in language production. However, one of the objectives of the course, and certainly a goal of the college-bound students themselves, was to increase the **accuracy** of their production, and in this regard we were not always successful.

4.4 The missing link: collocation

The reason that 'we don't usually use it that way' is explained with the idea of collocation. The three student-produced sentences are incorrect because they contain collocation errors. What is collocation? You might get a different definition from every linguist you asked because terminology is not yet fixed, but don't at this stage worry too much about what collocation is, or how it might be precisely defined. I have found it easier to work with this very simple definition: Two or more words that tend to occur together (collocate). Elsewhere in this book different kinds of collocations, and a more theoretical perspective, are discussed in more detail.

Even with my simple definition, it is easy to see immediately that collocations may be of several different types:

verb + object	*dispute findings*
adjective + noun	*unaccompanied minor*
verb + preposition	*engage in, hear about*
adverb + adjective + noun	*highly irregular situation*

Smadja points out that why these words occur together cannot easily be explained on semantic grounds, and the sentences produced by our IEP students are good examples of the problem. Returning to the *toxic snake* we can see that although the student may learn the grammatical collocation of *adjective+noun*, and may learn that 'the meaning' of *toxic* is *poisonous*, all of that information neither helps the student to **produce** the expected *poisonous snake*, nor, equally importantly, to **avoid** the non-standard/unacceptable *toxic snake*. The same is true for the *potent Ferrari*. One meaning of *potent* is powerful, and both are adjectives, but one does go – collocate – with *Ferrari* and the other does not. Similarly, *severed class* is another collocation error.

For the native speaker, knowledge of acceptable and unacceptable collocations is largely instinctive. This is demonstrated by the way most native speakers would automatically add exactly the same words to complete these phrases: *sibling* . . . . . . , *mitigating* . . . .

You almost certainly selected *sibling rivalry* and *mitigating circumstances*. In fact, it is quite difficult to think of alternatives to the 'obvious' answers which are plausible and likely.

Collocations may be strong – the presence of one word means you strongly expect the other word to be there too – or weak, when the collocates can vary a great deal. I have found it helpful to conceptualize collocations on a continuum like the one below. On such a continuum, units made of freely-combining words like *friendly dog* or *old car* would not be treated as collocations, nor would fixed expressions and idioms like *throw in the towel*. I treat as collocations those items that appear in the middle of this continuum, with stronger collocations to the right, and weaker collocations to the left.

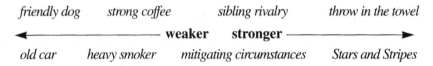

friendly dog	*strong coffee*	*sibling rivalry*	*throw in the towel*

◄——————————— **weaker**   **stronger** ———————————►

old car	*heavy smoker*	*mitigating circumstances*	*Stars and Stripes*

[Jane talks of what she 'treats as' collocations. This is wise; rather than getting involved in long discussions of what exactly is and is not a collocation, teachers need to make a pedagogical, rather than theoretical decision. Ed]

4.5 The need for guidance from the teacher

For the study of collocations to be successful, the teacher has the responsibility to direct learners' attention to the most useful collocations, those which hold high priority in the context of the curriculum. We should also discourage students from going overboard, and recording every collocation they meet. This means they must be discouraged from recording very weak items *(nice house, good vacation)*, or strong ones which are very unusual, and correspondingly probably not appropriate for most learners *(reduced to penury)*.

Not all vocabulary errors are collocation errors. Some are substitution or contextual errors, using the wrong word with the wrong meaning. Some examples of vocabulary errors of this type produced by our students are, *When I have children, I hope I will be very amorous with them*, and *Our trainers are very helpful and suggestive*. These students simply learned the wrong meaning, or the wrong context, for *amorous* and *suggestive*.

When one realizes that native speakers not only know an enormous number of individual words, but they also know much more about how these combine, or collocate, the burden of the L2 learner suddenly seems even greater. It may have seemed difficult enough for our students to learn the word *sibling*, but to learn also that native speakers use *sibling rivalry* and do not generally use *sibling competition* makes the task even more daunting. We suddenly realize the 20,000-word vocabulary forms only the rudimentary base of the native speaker's mental lexicon. This, combined with the 'word choice' errors the L2 learners make, despite contextualized presentation of new vocabulary, is evidence that ESL students need additional, explicit instruction in collocations. Swan reminds us that vocabulary 'will not take care of itself', and points out the pedagogic necessity of deliberately selecting, incorporating, and recycling high-priority vocabulary into classroom materials and activities. This point applies just as much, if not more, to collocations which students are less likely to notice unless guided towards the importance of collocation by their teachers.

After the initial *Aha!* feeling one has when realizing how much collocations come to bear upon language, the classroom teacher has to consider the question of just how to go about the explicit teaching of collocation. Today, in part due to technological advances, more research and resources than ever are available to help the classroom teacher specifically address the collocation 'problem'. Collocation has often been a source of student error; some teaching suggestions follow that can help students understand the idea of collocation and enable them to use collocations to their advantage in building their mental lexicons in a systematic way.

4.6 Make students aware of collocation

In some ways, it is a relief to bring collocations out of the closet, so to speak. Instead of feeling frustrated and a bit ineffectual when a student asks me, *But why don't Americans say 'mitigating situations'?* I can answer with something more than, *We just don't say it that way.* It is empowering for both the students and the teacher to be able to identify an area of difficulty, address it and provide a general, and generalizable, explanation. It is important to make students aware of collocations for this very reason. Listed below are ways classroom teachers can assist their students in taking control of this part of their language learning.

1. Teach students the word 'collocation'

Collocations exist in the students' L1, so, except for students of extremely limited proficiency, it really is not difficult for them to understand the concept. It is helpful to remind them that, just like their native language, the English language has some words that go together, and some that do not. Once explained, you can save a great deal of class time by using the term when appropriate.

2. Adapt books to include collocations

Currently, few textbooks for ESL students address collocations explicitly.

Modifying and adapting existing books is a good solution, and this can be accomplished fairly easily. If using vocabulary-builder books based on word-lists or roots and affixes, have students adapt them. Students can make notations about frequent collocations next to the word lists. Teachers should feel confident in supplying frequent collocations from their own knowledge of the English lexicon, but if desired, it's also possible to check some of the corpus-based references mentioned below.

3. Context and collocation notebooks

Within the specific area of vocabulary building, I have found it useful to present to the students 'the two C's' of *context* and *collocation*. When I first started presenting new words with only the collocations, this did not always help them avoid pitfalls with new vocabulary because individual words and multi-word items can operate within a restricted context as well as with particular collocates. For example, the following is a sample of some context and collocation information I gave to some students using Goodman's *Advancing Vocabulary Skills*, a book for native speakers and learners which we have at times used in our advanced reading and writing class.

Word	Special context?	Collocations
discretion (n)	(caution/privacy, authority, judgment)	at your/someone's discretion verbs: exercise ~ , handle sth with ~, use ~, leave to sb's ~ show ~ adj: complete/total/utmost ~

There are no service charges added to the bill. Tip at your discretion.
He handled the private matter with complete discretion.
The job applicants were hired at the discretion of the hiring committee.

facetious (adj)   (flippant – often negative)   noun: ~ remark

I wish Bill would stop making facetious remarks.

scrupulous (adj) (relating to honesty,   noun: ~ care, ~ attention
                  fairness, exactness)
John deals with the accounts and he's absolutely scrupulous.

What works especially well for this purpose is a stenographer's notebook. [used for taking US shorthand, Ed.] It's a portable size for recording vocabulary, and also comes ready-made with two columns that are ideally suited to record context and collocation in their respective places, following the initial word entry and definition. During one of the first class meetings, I model how to record the context and collocation of each word, and then for the remainder of the course, whenever we work specifically on vocabulary, I write the two headings, **Context** and **Collocation**, on the blackboard, and write the relevant notations under each heading as we work down the list. For

6. Really useful words

Some nouns do not have much meaning, so they nearly always have an adjective with them. In some ways they are more like part of the grammar of English than its vocabulary. If you want to use nouns like this naturally, you need to know lots of adjective collocates. Almost any noun headword which has a very long entry in a collocation dictionary is suitable for this activity, such as:

> *account, action, answer, approach, argument, behaviour, change, circumstances, condition, consequences, decision, difference, discussion, effect, feature, idea, information, interest, issue, manner, method, move, performance, plan, policy, position, problem, programme, project, question, reason, relationship, result, scheme, situation, solution, state, story, style, system, theme, theory, use, view, vision, way, work.*

As a simple five-minute activity, choose one of these words. Take six adjective collocations from a collocation dictionary and write them on the board, for example:

> *an embarrassing situation*   *a unique situation*
> *a bewildering situation*   *an extraordinary situation*
> *a tricky situation*   *a tense situation*

Ask learners to think of a real example of each from their own lives and write a sentence or tell a partner about some of the situations.

One reason these words are so common is because they are used in many different contexts. Specific examples suggest contexts; what context does each of these examples suggest:

> *tell a funny story*   *concoct an implausible story*
> *run a front page story*   *believe somebody's sob story*

With many of the nouns above, you may want to sort examples first (see Activity 7), then put some of the collocations into sentence frames which provide a context, such as:

> *If you want to . . . , you're more likely to succeed if you adopt a logical/ flexible/cautious approach. If you adopt a more . . . approach, you'll only . . . .*

> *One of the most controversial issues which is being discussed (in my country) at the moment is . . . . It's an issue which tends to divide. . . .*

This activity reminds us that teachers should keep language in the largest possible context or frame, rather than trying to break it down. The larger the frame, the more useful information, including grammatical collocations, is likely to be retained. This, in turn, means learners are more likely to store larger chunks and that they will make fewer mistakes when re-using the language themselves.

7. Sorting

Ask learners to work in groups and select items from a collocation dictionary entry using a 'rule'. For example, look up the verb *change* and find collocates which suggest 'quickly', such as: *abruptly, immediately, overnight.* Or look up the word *reason* and find adjectives which are negative in different ways, for example: *far-fetched, frivolous, perverse, sinister.*

Here are some more general 'rules' which you can use with many different words. Search for:

- verbs or adjectives which seem positive or negative
- adjectives which mean *big / strong / serious*
- adjectives which mean *small / slight / minor*
- verbs which mean something started / stopped
- verbs which mean something changed in a certain way

Many of these 'rules' work well with these words:

crisis, style, rules, view, marriage, image, strike, reform, hope, search, scheme, measures, solution, role, risk

8. Near synonyms

Take two or more words with similar meaning. For example:

injury   wound

Ask learners to look carefully at the adjective and verb collocates of both words in a collocation dictionary. The difference in the way similar words are used is often largely the difference in their collocational fields. Ask learners to translate some of the collocations into their own language; this will help learners build an understanding of how the English words are used. More advanced learners can use groups of words of similar meaning, for example:

1. answer, conclusion, explanation, result, solution
2. mistake, error, fault, problem, defect
3. instructions, guidelines, rules, regulations, directives
4. ability, talent, gift, skill, aptitude
5. pattern, shape, form, design, structure
6. document, report, file, article, story, account
7. task, job, work, career, occupation, profession
8. number, quantity, amount, size, dimensions, proportions

9. Rapid sorting

Give learners two nouns from a collocation dictionary, which they write on a piece of paper. Read out a selection of about 10/12 collocates from the entries. Students write the collocates in **one** or **both** lists as appropriate.

Try to choose **relatively new**, half-known words. If you choose words of similar meaning, you must be prepared to discuss possibilities and sort out possible confusion. Remember that collocation is about probabilities, not black and white choices. Here is an example:

ANSWER	REPLY
expect, supply, insist on	expect, send, insist on
have, appropriate, complete	appropriate, audible
detailed, final	detailed, pointed

If you want to wake up a sleepy class, you can turn this activity into real activity by having learners point to the left hand wall if the verb collocates with *answer*, the right hand wall if it collocates with *reply*, and both walls if the verb collocates with **both** nouns.

10. Five-word stories

Look up *order* and *examination* in a collocation dictionary. Find five verbs for each which suggest a 'story' if they are in a particular order like this:

place, get, process, despatch, receive **an order**
enter for, revise for, take, fail, re-sit **an examination**

You can do the same with any noun which suggests an extended process such as: *problem, product, relationship, research, system, letter, war, negotiations, job.*

11. Collecting collocations

Learners often do not realise **how many** words collocate with a word they already know. This means they do not get full value from the words they know. When an interesting noun comes up in class, read out a list of about 10 verbs which **may** collocate with it and ask learners to note all the **correct** collocates as you read. Use seven or eight correct words, particularly half-familiar words – again a collocation dictionary will provide you with a helpful list – and add two or three others which do **not** make correct collocations. This activity reminds us of the importance of negative evidence. It also provides an opportunity to remind learners of words they often overuse such as *do, make, have, take.* Make sure they note any **relatively new** words; perhaps in a 5-1 box. Choose the words you practise for particular classes. With a general course you might choose *money,* or with a specialist group *economy,* then use the following lists where the non-collocates are marked *:

money: borrow, change, earn, *gain, invest, make, *reduce, save, spend
economy: boost, *break, *do, expand, kick start, run, steer, stimulate

12. Translating collocations

When you are browsing a dictionary or reading a text with a class, you will often notice *verb + adjective + noun* collocations such as *earn a proper wage, modify the original proposal, take regular exercise.* Draw these to students' attention and ask them to translate them into their own language **as single units**. Doing this regularly will help students become more aware of collocation and less inclined to translate word-for-word.

13. As easy as possible

Learners work in small teams, two teams competing against another. Give each team a list of, say, 10 nouns which are headwords in a collocation dictionary. Choose these carefully, taking into account the class level, words met recently etc. Each group has about 10 minutes to prepare, using the dictionary. They list 5 collocates from the dictionary for each noun. Team A then say these one at a time for each headword to Team B who have to write the words down and try to guess the noun. The interest lies in the fact that collocates should be chosen so that **Team B's task is as easy as possible**.

If they guess a noun from one collocate, Team A scores 5 points, if they need two collocates, 4 points and so on. If they do not work out (not, we hope, 'guess') the headword when they have all five collocates, Team A scores 0 for that word. When Team A has gone though its 10 words, Team B does the same.

Notice the game is constructed so that the team which uses the **strongest** and/or **most frequent** collocates is likely to win, so there is a systematic element built into the design of the game. Here are some words which you can use to demonstrate how to choose words:

> **examination**: revise for, re-sit, pass, fail, take
> **language**: foreign, spoken, written, sign, strong
> **job**: apply for, look for, get, lose, hold down
> **rules**: obey, stick to, bend, explain, change
> **smell**: delicious, disgusting, awful, terrible, horrible
> **interested**: not remotely, extremely, seriously, vaguely, definitely

14. The collocation game

Choose a noun with a lot of verb or adjective collocates – again, a collocation dictionary is a big help. Tell the learners that all the words you read out collocate with the **same** noun, which they must try to guess. Learners write down the collocates you read out. When they think they know the noun, they stand up. Continue till everyone is standing. Check guesses. Repeat with a new word.

This activity only works properly if you choose the order of the words carefully, moving from **more general** words to **stronger** collocates. Make sure before you start that there is **one** word that means everyone will recognise the noun, so that the activity does not become unnecessarily frustrating for learners. Here are some examples:

1. plain, dark, white, bitter, milk, bar of	**chocolate**
2. collect, provide, volunteer, conceal, gather, withhold	**information**
3. test, advance, build, outline, put forward, corroborate	**a theory**
4. huge, growing, profitable, export, domestic, black	**market**
5. year, loss, allowance, bracket, haven, evasion	**tax**
6. cut, calculate, cover, minimise, meet, recover, amortise	**the cost of**

Example 3 is suitable for an English for Academic Purposes group, and Examples 4-6 for a business English group.

You can do the same thing with adverbs and adjectives or verbs:

7. fairly, relatively, ridiculously, comparatively, dead	**easy**
8. extremely, reasonably, remarkably, superbly, fighting	**fit**
9. upstairs, in luxury, alone, beyond your means, to a ripe old age	**live**
10. carefully, thoroughly, properly, closely, in minute detail	**examine**

After you have played this game several times, if you have a number of dictionaries, students can do the activity independently in small groups.

15. Noun + noun combinations

English word classes are unusually flexible, so verbs can be used as nouns, nouns as adjectives and so on. Even advanced learners do not always feel comfortable using *noun + noun* combinations, and may need to be reassured that these are standard English. Here are two sequences of such combinations which teachers can easily adapt into a collocation game such as collocation dominoes.

blank cheque – cheque book – book club – club sandwich – sandwich board – board room – room service – service charge – charge card

table top – top quality – quality time – time management – management course – course work – workshop – shop assistant – assistant manager

16. Exploring examples

Peter Sunderland (*Arena*, Issue 19) describes the advantages of exploring a group of examples rather than looking for distinctions of meaning, reflecting a point made by George Woolard in his chapter.

"I am increasingly coming to see no distinction between vocabulary and grammar lessons in my mind, replacing them with the belief that a lexical approach based on teaching chunks of language is of greater value to student and teacher. Correspondingly, the end product of my lessons is maximising the students' communicative power by exposing them to useful, real chunks of language.

An advanced class want to be able to use words other than *shine*. They recognise *glitter, glow, gleam* etc but have little idea of the distinguishing uses. Traditionally, there have been four ways of distinguishing uses:

1. Traditional standard dictionary definitions:

   glitter: sparkle with light
   gleam: glow or shine not very brightly
   glisten: gleam or shimmer, as a wet, oily surface does
   shimmer: gleam tremulously or glisten

These are of practically no use to EFL learners. As can be seen, the definitions are interchangeable and rely on each other.

2. Typical EFL dictionary definitions:

> **glitter**: shine in a sparkling way
> **gleam**: shine brightly as reflecting light or as very clean
> **glisten**: shimmer brightly as smooth, wet or oily
> **shimmer**: shine with a fairly unsteady light

These are slightly more helpful as all the definitions revolve around variations of *shine*.

3. Typical EFL dictionary distinguishing information:

> **glitter**: many little flashes
> **gleam**: reflect/clean
> **glisten**: wet/oily
> **shimmer**: unsteady, soft light

Better still; a little over-simplified, a sanitised version of the truth but more user-friendly.

4. Typical EFL dictionary examples:

> **glitter**: star, eyes, diamonds, career, prize, array
> **gleam**: white teeth, car (new), (eyes) with excitement, hair, (gold/black)
> **glisten**: sweat on the face, eyes (with tears), dew drops on grass
> **glimmer**: lights (in the distance), of success/hope/interest
> **shimmer**: moonlight on water
> **glow**: embers/ashes, skin/complexion with health, praise/tribute/
>   report/terms

This last approach is of greatest use. We go straight to the real, the probable, the typical and the frequent; **actual combinations of words** as the starting point. Students learn native-speaker phrases, and may or may not work back towards distinguishing definitions, like those in 3 above. As with native speakers, knowledge of the collocations may be enough to provide an instinct for what is correct. The basis of teaching and learning is observation of used language. This procedure recognises that it is often collocational field which distinguishes these groups of words which have similar meanings."

5.5 Exercises

1. Correcting common mistakes

There is a collocation mistake in each of these sentences. Correct them by looking up the word **in bold** in a collocation dictionary. All the mistakes are similar to those made by candidates in the First Certificate exam.

1. I was completely **disappointed** when I failed my exam.
2. When I did badly in the exam it was a strong **disappointment**.
3. When you decide what to study, you must make a planned **choice**.
4. The holiday I went on last year was a full **disaster**.
5. What happened next was a really **disaster**.
6. I'm afraid I would like to do a serious **complaint**.
7. If you want to lose weight, you need to make a **diet**.
8. Getting on a **diet** will help you.
9. If you are too fat, you need to miss some **weight**.
10. To improve your health you need to do some **sacrifices**.
11. If you want to be really fit, you need to make more **exercise**.
12. If you don't keep to your diet, you won't have the **result** you want.

This type of exercise is particularly useful as feedback after learners have done a piece of written work.

The following six exercises all focus on collocations where one of the words modifies the other, for example, *verb + adverb, adverb + adjective*. These exercises are useful and comparatively easy to write. It is important to remember, however, that activities and exercises which introduce collocations which **identify** or name a concept, for example, *verb + noun* collocations such as *make a mistake* or *propose a toast* are perhaps more important if learners are to build their lexicons in a way which is both systematic and balanced.

2. Verb + adverb

Some verbs collocate strongly with particular adverbs. Use each adverb once to complete these sentences. If in doubt, check the **verb** in a collocation dictionary.

categorically	*confidently*	*completely*	*flatly*	*fully*
legitimately	*hardly*	*readily*	*strongly*	*tentatively*

1. I'm sorry, I . . . . forgot to pass your message on.
2. He . . . . refused to help.
3. Oh it's you! I . . . . recognised you with your new haircut.
4. I . . . . recommend we wait until we have more information.
5. I . . . . admit I did not expect things to change so quickly.
6. I don't think you . . . . appreciate how serious the situation is.
7. She can . . . . claim that she had the idea before anyone else.
8. I . . . . deny that it was anything to do with me.
9. We . . . . expect to make as much profit this year as last.
10. Could I . . . . suggest it might be better to wait?

3. Alternatives to *very*

With many adjectives you want to use *very*, but there are lots of other words with a similar meaning which are stronger or more precise. For example:

highly qualified   *bitterly* disappointed

Use a collocation dictionary to add a word which means *very* to each of these:

1. . . . . exhausted	5. . . . . encouraged
2. . . . . disorganised	6. . . . . unexpected
3. . . . . handicapped	7. . . . . recommended
4. . . . . disillusioned	8. . . . . prepared

Now do the same with these:

1. . . . . greedy	7. . . . . grateful
2. . . . . honest	8. . . . . impractical
3. . . . . inaccurate	9. . . . . offensive
4. . . . . remarkable	10. . . . . ruthless
5. . . . . sceptical	11. . . . . sure
6. . . . . theoretical	12. . . . . unacceptable

When you put an adjective in your notebook, try to record a word with it which means *very*.

Often you can also find a word which means *a bit*, for example, *slightly* inaccurate, *somewhat* sceptical.

4. Verb + adverb phrase

Some adverb phrases strongly suggest one particular verb. Can you add the verb (in the correct form) to each of these? The clue is in the adverb phrase. If in doubt, look up the verbs in a collocation dictionary. You need to use each of these verbs once:

accept	*change*	*live*	*prove*	*refuse*
reject	*search*	*sign*	*spread*	*think*

1. The government . . . . *point-blank* to consider introducing new legislation.
2. The government has . . . . *out of hand* the possibility of changing the law.
3. Have you seen my briefcase anywhere? I've . . . . *high and low*, but I can't find it.
4. Everything's agreed; we're just waiting for them to . . . . *on the dotted line.*
5. When the news got out, it . . . . *like wildfire.*
6. This . . . . *beyond all shadow of doubt* that he did it.
7. I hope I will . . . . *to a ripe old age.*

8. The band's tour of Japan . . . . *in triumph* with a sell-out concert in Tokyo.

9. I see what you mean. We're obviously . . . . *along the same lines.*

10 It was years since I'd been there and the town had . . . . *out of all recognition.*

An exercise like this can be used to encourage learners to see that it is better to learn language in chunks. In this exercise, they need to learn the whole phrase, complete with the verb.

5. Adverb + adjective

Some *adverb + adjective* collocations are often fairly strong. Match each adverb in List 1 with an adjective in List 2. You should find all the answers in a collocation dictionary by looking up the adjectives.

List 1	**List 2**
1. delicately	a. associated with
2. closely	b. balanced
3. enthusiastically	c. chosen
4. highly	d. mistaken
5. carefully	e. overcrowded
6. ideally	f. qualified
7. badly	g. received
8. dangerously	h. situated

Now complete each of these sentences with one of the expressions:

1. The election is very . . . . at the moment. Either party could win.

2. The new production of 'Hamlet' was . . . . by the first night audience.

3. She's too . . . . for the job – we don't want someone with a degree.

4. The house is . . . . , ten minutes from the sea, and ten minutes to the mountains.

5. If you think I'm going to agree to that, you're . . . .

6. The disco was already . . . . when the fire started.

7. His words were . . . . to ensure they appealed to different sections of the audience.

8. The President has been . . . . the idea from the start, so he's very anxious that it is a success.

6. Adverb + adjective

Match the adverbs in List 1 with the adjectives in List 2. You should find all the answers in a collocation dictionary by looking up the adjectives.

List 1	**List 2**
1. bitterly	a. anticipated
2. strictly	b. available
3. lavishly	c. damaged
4. eagerly	d. disappointed
5. generously	e. illustrated
6. widely	f. influenced by
7. heavily	g. limited
8. extensively	h. rewarded

Now complete these texts using each of the expressions once:

1. Oasis's new tour was . . . . and tickets were
   supposed to be . . . . but in fact they were
   . . . . to two per person. I was . . . .
   that I couldn't get any tickets all.

2. A new . . . . biography of Princess Diana has just
   appeared. It seems to have been . . . . by interest
   in America. There are some new, rather personal photos, supplied by
   so-called friends of hers who have, no doubt, been . . . .
   for supplying personal details. Famous people often don't realise their
   reputation can be . . . . by so-called friends. I'm
   glad I'm not famous.

7. Adverb + adjective

Use each of these adverbs once to complete the examples. If in doubt, look up the **verbs** in a collocation dictionary.

absolutely	*densely*	*fatally*	*generally*
heavily	*hopelessly*	*ideally*	*narrowly*
richly	*severely*	*sorely*	*strictly*

1. 'Lord of the Flies' is still . . . . considered to be Golding's
   most successful book.
2. I'm . . . . tempted to keep the money – I could do with some
   extra at the moment.
3. Supplies at this low price are . . . . limited.
4. Central California is one of the most . . . . populated parts of
   the United States.
5. I was . . . . appalled to hear they were discussing bringing
   back the death penalty.
6. The house is . . . . situated – on the coast, near the city and
   surrounded by beautiful mountains.

7. I realised I'd taken the wrong road, and when I came to the second roundabout, I was . . . . confused.

8. Everyone was delighted at her success, which was . . . . deserved.

9. The theory turned out to be . . . . flawed.

10. Exporters who do not have foreign language skills are . . . . handicapped.

11. All the news coming from the region is . . . . censored.

12. The polls suggest that the government will be . . . . defeated in the referendum.

8. Synonyms

Use a collocation dictionary to find another word similar in meaning to the word in **bold**:

1. Rumours are **rife** or . . . .
2. You can **get into** a row or get . . . . . . **in** one.
3. You **grow up** in a neighbourhood or are . . . . **up** in it.
4. News can **slip out** or . . . . . **out**.
5. You can see something **clearly** or . . . .
6. You can **make** a guess or . . . . . . a guess.
7. You can **galvanise** or . . . . . . public opinion.
8. You can **demand** or . . . . . . certain minimum qualifications.

This type of exercise, which gives learners alternative ways of saying the same thing, is only suitable for advanced learners.

9. Opposites

Use a collocation dictionary to find a word which is opposite in meaning to the one in **bold**:

1. You can **dismiss** or . . . . . . employees.

2. You can **impose** or . . . . . . an embargo on a country.

3. We thought that crossing the Kalahari would be a fairly **dangerous** journey, but it turned out to be quite . . . .

4. If somebody is stealing things at work, you can **instigate** an investigation and then . . . . . . it if it is causing too much trouble.

5. Are you the sort of person who **follows** or . . . . . . instructions?

6. John is the **perfect** guest, but Tony is one of the most . . . . . . guests I have ever entertained.

7. You can either **loosen** your grip on something or . . . . . . it.

8. I had an accident in my car last week. There was some **slight** damage to the front of the car, but the damage to the back was . . . .

Sometimes the opposite of *weak* is *strong*: *weak/strong tea* but the opposite of *strong cheese* is *mild cheese* not *weak cheese*, so once again remind learners of the need to learn words in collocations or larger chunks.

10. The missing verb

What are the missing verbs in the following collocations? The same verb completes all three examples. If in doubt, check the nouns in a collocation dictionary. Notice how important it is to learn words in phrases rather than single words.

1. . . . . a mistake   4. . . . . panic
                 a statement   a problem
                 an observation   embarrassment

2. . . . . to a complete standstill   5. . . . . danger
                 to an understanding   an accident
                 to a decision   a question

3. . . . . concern
                 embarrassment
                 fear

11. Interesting adjectives – 1

Complete the sentences using each of these adjectives once. In each case one of the adjectives is the fairly obvious choice.

bitter	*embarrassing*	*extensive*	*genuine*	*inspired*	*powerful*
safe	*remarkable*	*sound*	*strict*	*wide*	*wild*

1. It's a . . . . assumption that he will pass the exam easily.

2. Your parents gave you very . . . . advice. You'd be wise to listen to them.

3. I found myself in the . . . . position of having to apologise again.

4. It was a . . . . disappointment when I couldn't get onto the course I liked most.

5. Our holiday in Iceland was an . . . . choice. We enjoyed every minute of it.

6. It's a . . . . coincidence, but four out of five members of the team come from the same village.

7. The old part of the town suffered . . . . damage in the war.

8. The team won the championship by a very . . . . margin, the biggest ever.

9. He has a . . . . gift for helping other people.

10. If you're serious about losing weight, you need to go on a . . . . diet.

11. The performance was absolutely wonderful and greeted with . . . . . .
    enthusiasm by a large audience.

12. There is a . . . . argument for spending a year at work before
    you go to university.

12. Interesting adjectives – 2

You don't want to use the same few adjectives all the time: *a big
house/problem, an interesting job/person/book.* When you learn a noun, it is
always a good idea to learn at least one adjective which you can use to make
the noun stronger.

Add one or more of these adjectives to each of the nouns below. Sometimes
more than one is possible. If you are in doubt, check in your dictionary.

complete	*great*	*excellent*
heavy	*serious*	*total*
special	*strong*	*successful*

1. . . . . advantage
2. . . . . accident
3. . . . . agreement
4. . . . . ban
5. . . . . career
6. . . . . complaint
7. . . . . confusion
8. . . . . consequences
9. . . . . defeat
10. . . . . doubts
11. . . . . emphasis
12. . . . . example
13. . . . . feature
14. . . . . flavour

Exercises like this, which do not have unique, 'correct' answers need to be
used carefully so that they help rather than confuse learners.

13. Odd verb out

One verb in each line does not collocate with the noun. Cross out the one
which does not fit.

1. accept, act on, disregard, follow, ignore, make, solicit, take   ADVICE

2. come up with, do, expect, get, require, supply   AN ANSWER

3. build up, close down, set up, put off, take over, wind up   A BUSINESS

4. deal with, do, examine, ignore, reject, respond to   A COMPLAINT

5. accept, answer, come in for, give rise to, make, reject   CRITICISM

6. describe, do, enjoy, have, recall, share   AN EXPERIENCE

7. crash, finish, hire, park, repair, run, service, start, write off   A CAR

8. arrange, do, gatecrash, go to, have, throw   A PARTY

Now try these more difficult words:

1. acclaim, disparage, exaggerate, praise, reduce   AN ACHIEVEMENT

2. come to, decide, endorse, implement, reach, sign   AN AGREEMENT

3. analyse, determine, establish, make, study, trace   THE CAUSE

4. cause, compensate for, outweigh, realise   THE DISADVANTAGE(S)

5. classify, collate, deny, gather, organise, provide, withhold   MATERIAL

6. acknowledge, answer, create, meet, put, respond to   A NEED

7. announce, condemn, endorse, moderate, move, relax   A POLICY

8. adopt, apply, do, establish, propose, test, work out   A FORMULA

In No 8, which verbs suggest a *chemical/mathematical formula*, and which suggest a more general plan?

Notice that some of the most useful nouns are rather general words which do not carry very much meaning: *answer, changes, cause, policy*. Words like this are often used with a verb with a very precise meaning, and often with an adjective too in phrases like *act on professional advice, introduce radical changes, sign a provisional agreement, withhold sensitive material.*

14. Short paragraphs

1. Look up *news* in a collocation dictionary. Then try to complete this short text:

   A hundred years ago news was slow to . . . . in. Today as soon as news . . . . , it is flashed across the world by satellite. It is almost impossible for governments to . . . . news. No matter what they do to stop it . . . . , it will always . . . . out.

2. Look up *emergency*. Then try to complete this short text:

   Emergencies can never be . . . . When they take . . . . , the emergency services swing into action. As part of their everyday work, they . . . . . . for an emergency so that when one . . . . , they are ready for all eventualities. Unfortunately, ... emergencies happen all the time and cannot be . . . . , even with the best planning.

3. Look up *hair*. Then try to complete this short text:

   Sandra had dull . . . . . hair. She had tried every kind of shampoo. She had tried . . . . . it a different colour. She had even . . . . . it pure white just like Annie Lennox. Eventually, she had it all . . . . . off – start from scratch, she said. But it grew back, the same . . . . . straggly hair she had hated even from childhood.

To prepare students to write an essay, first ask them to write a paragraph similar to those above using five or six collocations of an important noun they will need for the essay.

15. Words into groups

Match each of these nouns to one of the **groups** of verbs. Remember, **all** the verbs in the group must collocate with the noun.

    attack   battle   dispute   fight   struggle   war

Group A: avoid, get into, pick, provoke, start, win

Group B: declare, go to, lead to, prolong, wage, win

Group C: be engaged in, continue, face, give up, join, take up

Group D: be vulnerable to, carry out, launch, mount, resist, step up

Group E: fight, force, go into, lose, win

Group F: aggravate, get involved in, intervene in, put an end to, resolve

Now do the same with these:

    fine   penalty   punishment   sentence   discipline

Group A: heavy, lenient, suspended, life, long, reduced

Group B: harsh, heavy, severe, death, stiff, huge

Group C: heavy, hefty, immediate, on-the-spot, stiff, token

Group D: effective, firm, strict, slack, poor, excessive

Group E: appropriate, brutal, capital, fit, lenient, harsh

16. Sentence adverbs

Put the following sentence adverbs into the sentences below.

    in fairness   in theory   in practice
    in retrospect   in other words   in particular

1. It's a good idea . . . . , but it will never work . . . .

2. I decided to leave school at sixteen. . . . . , it was the wrong decision. I should have stayed on and gone to university.

3. The destruction of the rain forests is a disaster, although, ... , politicians are starting to take it more seriously.

4. There are many problems with the present Health Service. . . . . , there are simply not enough hospital beds.

5. The situation is getting worse and worse. . . . . , we have no choice – things have to change and change soon!

Remember, discourse markers – phrases which help the reader through the text – are one kind of collocation which is frequently under-represented in teaching materials. Learners need practice of this kind of language if they are to develop an adequate lexicon for writing.

5.6 Your own exercises

If you write your own exercises using a collocation dictionary and copying one of the above formats, be warned that collocation is never as simple as it seems – sometimes the adverb must come in front of the verb, sometimes it must come after, and sometimes either position is possible with very similar meanings. Some *adjective + noun* or *verb + noun* combinations are much more common if they are used in the negative; perhaps some of the verbs are used with the headword mostly when it is literal, others mostly when it is more metaphorical. Very rarely are the lines between two 'different' uses of this kind clear; one use tends to overlap and merge into another – that is how real language works. Although writing exercises can be very frustrating, it is one of the best ways you can yourself develop a clearer understanding of collocation and in turn help your learners to notice, record and learn language from the texts they read in a way which builds their mental lexicons efficiently and systematically.

Finally, two warnings. You need to pay special attention to:

• General nouns, which are common and useful, which have little meaning on their own, but very wide collocation fields [See activity 6, p 101]. Learners think they 'know' these words, but they are a source of many mistakes when learners (mis-)use them in speech and writing.

• De-lexicalised verbs such as *do, make, put, keep, get, have*, which learners overuse when they do not know the appropriate verb collocate. They need to learn both which can be used with a particular noun, and, perhaps more importantly, which **cannot** be used with a particular noun *(*do a complaint, *make a hard diet)*.

In addition to the activities and exercises discussed in this chapter, many of the 45 Activities and 30 Exercise-types discussed in Chapters 6 and 7 of *Implementing the Lexical Approach* focus on collocations, and many familiar activities either already have, or can easily be adapted to have, a collocational focus.

5.7 Summary

All of the contributors to this book stress the importance of making learners more aware of the phrasal nature of language. The single most important kind of multi-word item is collocation. The single most important kind of collocation is the type which names a concept, usually *verb + noun (move house)* or *verb + adjective + noun (take the wrong turning)*. Finally, the single most important contribution the teacher can make to ensuring that input becomes intake, is ensuring that learners **notice** the collocations and other phrases in the input language. This involves an important change of perspective for many teachers, particularly those used to emphasising the language that students produce. We now recognise that it is noticing the input language which is crucial to expanding learners' mental lexicons. At the same time, teachers and learners expect to produce language in class, and any successful methodology needs to maintain involvement and motivation. For these reasons alone, productive activities and exercises are important. A balanced learning programme also involves quiet reflection and homework which helps to reinforce input. Teachers should remember, however, that **all** activities and exercises should be designed to support the central activity of encouraging learners to notice language in ways which maximise the chance of input being retained as long-term intake.

Discussion questions

Think of a vocabulary activity you use regularly in class. How can you adapt it so that it focusses on collocations rather than single words?

Do you think your learners learn most of their vocabulary in class or outside the classroom? What do you do in class to ensure that they can acquire collocations and phrases from the language they meet outside the classroom?

How would you introduce the idea of collocation to a class who had never met the idea before?

Chapter 6

Calloway's code

O. Henry

As a light interlude before the more theoretical part of this book, readers may enjoy this short story. It is about a hundred years old and, printed here in its original form, the vocabulary and style seem very dated. Surprisingly, however, it touches directly on the content of this book. There is a short commentary at the end of the chapter, but initially readers are invited to enjoy the linguistic skills of two journalists, Calloway (the encoder) and Vesey (the de-coder). Between them, they put fixed collocations to highly creative use.

The *New York Enterprise* sent H. B. Calloway as special correspondent to the Russo-Japanese-Portsmouth war.

For two months Calloway hung about Yokohama and Tokyo, shaking dice with other correspondents for drinks of rickshaws – oh no, that's something you ride in; anyway he wasn't earning the salary that his paper was paying him. But that was not Calloway's fault. The little brown men who held the strings of Fate between their fingers were not ready for the readers of the *Enterprise* to season their breakfast bacon and eggs with the battles of the descendants of the gods.

But soon the column of correspondents that were to go out with the First Army tightened their field-glass belts and went down to the Yalu with Kuroki. Calloway was one of these.

Now, this is no history of the battle of the Yalu River. That has been told in detail by the correspondents who gazed at the shrapnel smoke rings from a distance of three miles. But, for justice's sake, let it be understood that the Japanese commander prohibited a nearer view.

Calloway's feat was accomplished before the battle. What he did was to furnish the *Enterprise* with the biggest beat of the war. That paper published exclusively and in detail the news of the attack on the lines of the Russian general Zassulitch on the same day that it was made. No other paper printed a word about it for two days afterwards, except a London paper, whose account was absolutely incorrect and untrue.

Calloway did this in face of the fact that General Kuroki was making his moves and laying his plans with the profoundest secrecy as far as the world outside his camps was concerned. The correspondents were forbidden to send out any news whatever of his plans; and every message that was allowed on the wires was censored with rigid severity.

The correspondent for the London paper handed in a cablegram describing Kuroki's plans; but as it was wrong from beginning to end the censor grinned and let it go through.

So there they were – Kuroki on one side of the Yalu with forty-two thousand infantry, five thousand cavalry, and a hundred and twenty-four guns. On the other side, Zassulitch waited for him with only twenty-three thousand men, and with a long stretch of river to guard. And Calloway had got hold of some important inside information that he knew would bring the *Enterprise* staff around a cablegram as thick as flies around a Park Row lemonade stand. If he could only get that message past the censor – the new censor who had arrived and taken his post that day.

Calloway did the obviously proper thing. He lit his pipe and sat down on a gun carriage to think it over. And there we must leave him; for the rest of the story belongs to Vesey, a sixteen-dollar-a-week reporter on the *Enterprise.*

Calloway's cablegram was handed to the managing editor at four o'clock in the afternoon. He read it three times; and then drew a pocket mirror from a pigeon-hole in his desk, and looked at his reflection carefully. Then he went over to the desk of Boyd, his assistant (he was usually called Boyd when he wanted him), and laid the cablegram before him.

'It's from Calloway,' he said. 'See what you make of it.'

The message was dated at Wi-ju, and these were the words of it:

'Foregone preconcerted rash witching goes muffled rumour mine dark silent unfortunate richmond existing great hotly brute select mooted parlous beggars ye angel incontrovertible.'

Boyd read it twice.

'It's either a cipher or a sunstroke,' said he.

'Ever hear of anything like a code in the office – a secret code?' asked the ME, who had held his desk for only two years. Managing editors come and go.

'None except the vernacular that the lady specials write in,' said Boyd. 'Couldn't be an acrostic, could it?'

'I thought of that,' said the ME, 'but the beginning letters contained only four vowels. It must be a code of some sort.'

'Try 'em in groups,' suggested Boyd. 'Let's see – "Rash witching goes"– not with me it doesn't. "Muffled rumour mine" – must have an underground wire. "Dark silent unfortunate richmond" – no reason why he should knock that town so hard. "Existing great hotly" – no, that doesn't pan out. I'll call Scott.'

The city editor came in a hurry, and tried his luck. A city editor must know something about everything; so Scott knew a little about cipher-writing.

'It may be what is called an inverted alphabet cipher,' said he. 'I'll try that. "R" seems to be the oftenest used initial letter, with the exception of "m". Assuming "r" to mean "e", the most frequently used letter, we transpose the letters – so.'

Scott worked rapidly with his pencil for two minutes; and then showed the first word according to his reading – the word 'Scejtzez'. 'Great!'cried Boyd. 'It's a charade. My first is a Russian general. Go on, Scott.'

'No, that won't work,' said the city editor. 'It's undoubtedly a code. It's impossible to read it without the key. Has the office ever used a cipher code?'

'Just what I was asking,' said the ME. 'Hustle everybody up that ought to know. We must get at it some way. Calloway has evidently got hold of something big, and the censor has put the screws on, or he wouldn't have cabled in a lot of chop suey like this.'

Throughout the office of the *Enterprise* a drag-net was sent, hauling in such members of staff as would be likely to know of a code, past or present, by reason of their wisdom, information, natural intelligence, or length of servitude. They got together in a group in the city room, with the ME in the centre. No one had heard of a code. All began to explain to the head investigator that newspapers never use a code, anyhow – that is a cipher code. Of course the Associated Press stuff is a sort of code – an abbreviation, rather – but . . . .

The ME knew all that, and said so. He asked each man how long he had worked on the paper. Not one of them had drawn pay from an *Enterprise* envelope for longer than six years.

Calloway had been on the paper twelve years.

'Try old Heffelbauer,' said the ME. 'He was here when Park Row was a potato patch.'

Heffelbauer was an institution. He was half janitor, half handy-man about the office, and half watchman – thus becoming the peer of thirteen and one-half tailors. Sent for, he came, radiating his nationality.

'Heffelbauer,' said the ME, 'did you ever hear a code belonging to the office a long time ago – a private code? You know what a code is, don't you?'

'Yah,' said Heffelbauer, 'Sure I know vat a code is. Yah, apout dwelf or fifteen year ago der office had a code. Der reborters in der city-room haf it here.'

'Ah!' said the ME, 'We're getting on the trail now. Where was it kept, Heffelbauer? What do you know about it?'

'Somedimes,' said the retainer, 'dey keep it in der little room behind der library room.'

'Can you find it?' asked the ME eagerly. 'Do you know where it is?'

'Mein Gott!' said Heffelbauer. 'How long do you dink a code live? Der reborters call him a maskeet. But von day he butt mit his head der editor, und – 'Oh, he's talking about a goat,' said Boyd. 'Get out, Heffelbauer.'

Again discomfited, the concerted wit and resources of the *Enterprise* huddled around Calloway's puzzle, considering its mysterious words in vain.

Then Vesey came in.

Vesey was the youngest reporter. He had a thirty-two-inch chest and wore a number fourteen collar; but his bright Scotch plaid suit gave him a presence and conferred no obscurity upon his whereabouts. He wore his hat in such a position that people followed him about to see him take it off, convinced that it must be hung upon a peg driven into the back of his head. He was never without an immense, knotted, hard-wood cane with a German-silver tip on its crooked handle. Vesey was the best photograph hustler in the office. Scott said it was because no living human being could resist the personal triumph it was to hand his picture over to Vesey. Vesey always wrote his own news stories, except the big ones, which were sent to the re-write men. Add to this fact that among all the inhabitants, temples, and groves of this earth nothing existed that could abash Vesey, and his dim sketch is concluded.

Vesey butted into the circle of cipher readers very much as Heffelbauer's 'code' would have done, and asked what was up. Someone explained, with the touch of half-familiar condescension that they always used towards him. Vesey reached out and took the cablegram from the ME's hand. Under the protection of some special Providence, he was always doing appalling things like that, and coming off unscathed.

'It's a code,' said Vesey. 'Anybody got the key?'

'The office has no code,' said Boyd, reaching for the message. Vesey held to it.

'Then old Calloway expects us to read it anyhow,' said he. 'He's up a tree, or something and he's made this up so as to get it by the censor. It's up to us. Gee! I wish they had sent me, too. Say – we can't afford to fall down on our end of it. "Foregone, preconcerted, rash, witching" – h'm.'

Vesey sat down on a table corner and began to whistle softly, frowning at the cablegram.

'Let's have it, please,' said the ME. 'We've got to get to work on it.'

'I believe I've got a line on it,' said Vesey. 'Give me ten minutes.'

He walked up to his desk, threw his hat into a wastebasket, spread out flat on his chest like a gorgeous lizard, and started his pencil going. The wit and wisdom of the *Enterprise* remained in a loose group, and smiled at one another, nodding their heads toward Vesey. Then they began to exchange their theories about the cipher.

It took Vesey exactly fifteen minutes. He brought to the ME a pad with the code-key written on it.

'I felt the swing of it as soon as I saw it,' said Vesey. 'Hurrah for old Calloway! He's done the Japs and every paper in town that prints literature instead of news. Take a look at that.'

Thus had Vesey set forth the reading of the code:

Foregone – conclusion
Preconcerted – arrangement
Rash – act
Witching – hour of midnight
Goes – without saying
Muffled – report
Rumour – hath it

Mine – host
Dark – horse
Silent – majority
Unfortunate – pedestrians
Richmond – in the field
Existing – conditions
Great – White Way
Hotly – contested
Brute – force
Select – few
Mooted – question
Parlous – times
Beggars – description
Ye – correspondents
Angel – unawares
Incontrovertible – fact

'It's simply newspaper English,' explained Vesey. 'I've been reporting on the *Enterprise* long enough to know it by heart. Old Calloway gives us the cue word, and we use the word that naturally follows it just as we use 'em in the paper. Read it over, and you'll see how pat they drop into their places. Now, here's the message he intended us to get.'

Vesey handed out another sheet of paper.

> Concluded arrangement to act at hour of midnight without saying. Report hath it that a large body of cavalry and an overwhelming force of infantry will be thrown into the field. Conditions white. Way contested by only a small force. Question the *Times* description. Its correspondent is unaware of the facts.

'Great stuff!' cried Boyd excitedly. 'Kuroki crosses the Yalu tonight and attacks. Oh, we won't do a thing to the sheets that make up with Addison's essays, real estate transfers, and bowling scores!'

FOOTNOTE

Mr Vesey afterwards explained that the logical journalistic complement of the word 'unfortunate' was once the word 'victim'. But, since the automobile became so popular, the correct following word is now 'pedestrians'. Of course, in Calloway's code it meant 'infantry'.

'Mr Vesey,' said the ME, with his jollying-which-you-should-regard-a-favour manner, 'you have cast a serious reflection upon the literary standards of the paper that employs you. You have also assisted materially in giving us the biggest "beat" of the year. I will let you know in a day or two whether you are to be discharged or retained at a larger salary. Somebody send Ames to me.'

Ames was the king-pin, the snowy-petalled marguerite, the star-bright looloo of the re-write men. He saw attempted murder in the pains of green-apple colic, cyclones in the summer zephyr, lost children in every top-spinning

most teachers and students think of as idioms are those which are **both** fairly fixed **and** non-literal. With a narrow definition like that, idioms are a fairly small part of the total lexicon, and from a language teaching perspective they can safely be left to more advanced learners. Once we understand idiomaticity in its wider meaning – chunks which have **some degree** of fixedness, and perhaps **some degree** of non-literalness, it is clear that idioms are a central part of the lexicon and important for learners at all levels. John Sinclair, describing the early work by the team constructing the Cobuild dictionaries, writes:

> The principle of idiom is that a language user has available to him or her a large number of semi-preconstructed phrases that constitute single choices, even though they might appear to be analysable into segments. ...The overwhelming nature of [the corpus] evidence leads us to elevate the principle of idiom from being a rather minor feature, compared with grammar, to being at least as important as grammar in the explanation of how meaning arises in text.

> ...Just as it is misleading and unrevealing to subject *of course* to grammatical analysis, it is unhelpful to attempt to analyse grammatically any portion of text which appears to be constructed on the idiom principle.

Within this wider definition, all of the following, while not idioms in the traditional sense, exhibit some degree of idiomaticity:

That's neither here nor there.
Well, I mustn't keep you.
I see what you mean.
Take it or leave it.
playing for time
signed, sealed and delivered
going backward and forwards
a very cool reception
take the earliest possible opportunity to . . .
a heavy-handed approach to the problem
heavy rain

As examples such as *a cool reception, heavy rain, take the opportunity to* show, collocation is part of the overall spectrum of idiomaticity. As Sinclair observes:

> Collocation illustrates the idiom principle. On some occasions words appear to be chosen in pairs or groups and these are not necessarily adjacent.

Chitra Fernando, whose book *Idioms and Idiomaticity* is perhaps the best academic survey of this area of language, states: "Collocations are at the lower end of the idiomaticity scale being only weak realisations of the idiom principle." Very strong collocations, where you can hardly imagine any other use of one of the partner-words, are a kind of idiom: *We had a blazing row/argument.* Some collocations permit very limited choice: *The whole story/event was tinged with sadness/regret* (and not much else). But the vast majority of collocations, although part of the spectrum of idiomaticity, are not so restricted. Partner-words often combine freely with many other words, and the slots in a collocation can each be filled in many different ways. The same group of words may, therefore, be treated as both an idiom and a collocation but the **focus** of the two descriptions is rather different. Idioms focus mainly on the **meaning** of the whole, while collocation is concerned with **combinations** of words which do or do not occur.

This distinction is used in this book, but our main focus is firmly on 'words and the company they keep', although it is helpful to remember that this is part of the wider question of idiomaticity. We look now at how the term 'collocation' covers many different kinds of multi-word items.

7.5 Collocation

Collocation is the way in which words co-occur in natural text in statistically significant ways. It sounds an innocent definition, but one very important point needs to be made: collocation is about the way words naturally co-occur in what David Brazil brilliantly called 'used language'. Collocations are **not** words which we, in some sense, 'put together', they co-occur naturally, and the first task of the language teacher is to ensure that they are not unnecessarily taken apart in the classroom. If words occur together, learners need to notice that co-occurrence and, if they are to be recorded in a vocabulary book, the words should be recorded together, a point already made by several contributors.

In most classes learners will already know many individual words, so in these circumstances, they may need to learn about 'putting them together' in standard collocations, but this is part of the necessary artificiality of language teaching. It would unquestionably be better if learners had acquired the words together as a single chunk – a single choice – in the first place. If you learn *initial reaction* (one item) it is easy to split the chunk apart, and acquire *initial* and *reaction*, two more items. If you learn the two words separately, you must also learn a third item, the correct collocation. Separating collocations into their component words is easy; it is considerably more difficult to put words together to form natural collocations. Peter Howarth has pointed out that knowing which words **do** go with which, **and** which do not is a major problem for learners:

> It may be claimed that the problem facing the non-native writer or speaker is knowing which of a range of collocational options are restricted and which are free. ...[the] significance [of the data] lies in the way in which specific collocations might be predicted by

analogy, but are arbitrarily blocked by usage, and clearly they are the kind of phenomenon likely to confound learners. ...It is the gaps in collocability that are arbitrary.

Learners need to notice words with the words with which they naturally occur. They need guidance on what can be generalised, and, crucially, guidance from teachers on the all-important gaps – collocations which learners may expect to be possible, perhaps by analogy with their own language, or apparent synonymy within English – *wage war* but not **wage conflict, *wage battle* – but which are blocked by usage. There is a strong case to be made for introducing the term 'blocked collocation' to learners, and encouraging them to note such 'impossible' combinations by asking them to record and then indicate their non-acceptability by crossing through or 'cancelling' them.

When teachers help learners put words together, it is partly because learners broke the natural language they met down too far in the first place, either on an intuitive basis of what would make it easier, or, more embarrassingly, because teachers have encouraged them to notice and to record 'new words'. The larger the chunks are which learners originally acquire, the easier the task of re-producing natural language later. The message to teachers is clear: don't break language down too far in the false hope of simplifying; your efforts, even if successful in the short term, are almost certainly counterproductive in terms of long-term acquisition.

Different kinds of collocation

If we define collocation as the way words occur together, it is easy to see that the definition is very wide, and will cover many different kinds of item. Certainly, all of the following are collocations in the sense that we readily recognise that these groups of words are regularly found together:

1. *a difficult decision* (adjective + noun)
2. *submit a report* (verb + noun)
3. *radio station* (noun + noun)
4. *examine thoroughly* (verb + adverb)
5. *extremely inconvenient* (adverb + adjective)
6. *revise the original plan* (verb + adjective + noun)
7. *the fog closed in* (noun + verb)
8. *To put it another way* (discourse marker)
9. *a few years ago* (multi-word prepositional phrase)
10. *turn in* (phrasal verb)
11. *aware of* (adjective + preposition)
12. *fire escape* (compound noun)
13. *backwards and forwards* (binomial)
14. *hook, line and sinker* (trinomial)
15. *On the other hand* (fixed phrase)
16. *A sort of . . .* (incomplete fixed phrase)

17. *Not half!* (fixed expression)
18. *See you later/tomorrow/on Monday.* (semi-fixed expression)
19. *Too many cooks . . .* (part of a proverb)
20. *To be or not to be . . .* (part of a quotation)

From the language teaching point of view, many of these are familiar and have formed a regular part of classroom teaching materials. The contributors to this book focus almost exclusively on those kinds of collocations which are relatively new in language teaching and which are only now finding their way into materials. There is extensive discussion of types 1 to 7 in the above list, with some references to types 8 and 9, but relatively little mention of the older, familiar types of multi-word item. George Woolard earlier suggested reasons for restricting the use of the term 'collocation' for learners to the newer kinds. [See p 29.]

Lexical and grammatical collocations

Some writers distinguish between lexical collocations such as *suggest an alternative, an evasive answer*, and grammatical collocations such as *aware of, step into*. In this terminology, lexical collocations combine two equal lexical components (open class words), while grammatical collocations combine a lexical word, typically a noun, verb or adjective, with a grammatical word (one open class word and one closed class word). Within this framework, phrasal verbs are neither more nor less than grammatical collocations. The main focus in this book is on lexical collocations, though it is worth noting that learners would often be well advised to record more than simple two-word combinations. It is better to record phrases such as *put the meeting off until . . .* , so they include **both** lexical words and grammatical words which are often used together.

Similarly, recording grammatical collocations such as *aware of, interested in* is unsatisfactory as these combinations are **never** used without at least one more word, so it makes more (collocational) sense to teach combinations such as *aware of the problems, interested in football*, choosing typical examples of how the words are used in a slightly larger context. Throughout this book teachers are repeatedly urged to encourage students to record language in larger chunks, and to keep at least part of the context in which the word actually occurred as part of what is recorded. A comment of Svetlana Ter-Minasova's *(Language, Linguistics and Life)* is typical:

> Foreign learners must keep in mind that they should learn words
> not through translations of their meanings (that is, reference to bits
> of reality and concepts), but in their most natural, habitual contexts,
> typical of the target language.

Collocations are often idiomatic

Some collocations appear superficially 'logical' – *open the window, play tennis, break your leg* – but many, although very familiar and which we easily think of as 'obvious' or 'sounding right', are conventional. Notice how the meanings of the verbs in the following differ considerably from the three earlier examples: *open a meeting* (why not *start*), *play some music* (why not *make*), *break the silence* (why not *interrupt* or *explode*). In fact, very few collocations are truly self-evident or literal; there is a partially non-literal, metaphorical or idiomatic element to most collocations. This means that, like other idioms, they are not **fully** predictable from their component words.

TASK

Think of three nouns which can follow the verb *answer* which intermediate learners are unlikely to know and which they probably would not guess.

Think of three nouns which can be used with the adjective *strong* but where the meaning of *strong* is quite different in each case.

How many things can you *open* where the opening is not like opening a door?

Did you think of *answer an enquiry, a letter, the door, the charge that . . .*? It is easy to see that the translations of these expressions into another language could very well involve a different verb in each expression. Similarly, with *strong opinions, wind, coffee, cheese,* or *opening a bottle, a letter, a meeting.*

Because some collocations are so familiar, it is easy to think they are obvious when they are, in fact, highly idiomatic. In an article on phraseology, Peter Howarth refers in passing to 'completely transparent collocations such as *have children*' but although there may be little difficulty guessing what this combination of words means, it may present learners with considerable problems from a productive point of view. Note first the difference between *She has a baby* and *She's having a baby*; changing the grammar changes the meaning of the verb. If you consider the expression from the perspective of a Swedish learner, for example, the first is *Hon har ett barn* mirroring the structure of the English exactly, although *barn* is closer to the English word *child*; but the second is *Hon vänta barn*, literally *She is waiting for (a) child*, closer to English *She's expecting a child*, though even here *She's expecting a baby* is closer to the Swedish. Grammar and words are in complex interplay, so that apparently transparent collocations hold many potential pitfalls for the learner.

Ter-Minasova gives another example from the perspective of Russian learners of English: the introduction to the *BBI Combinatory Dictionary* sees *open the gate* as a free collocation, allowing substitutions such as *lock the gate, open the door*, etc which should cause few problems for learners, but she comments:

> Many word-combinations look deceptively free within their own language, and their non-freedom only becomes obvious when they have to be translated into another language. The free, variable *open the gate* is, indeed free and variable within its own – English – language. However it looks much less free in the eyes of a Russian learner who tries to express the equivalent meaning. ...The Russian equivalent of *to open* is presented by quite a variety of verbs in Russian-English dictionaries *open, discover, clear, bare, reveal . . .* and the Russian word for *gate* has only the plural form.

The point for teachers is that even the simplest of collocations may contain difficulties for learners, and some comment to make learners aware of problems, including the 'blocked' collocations discussed earlier, may be necessary. It may even be that unexpected combinations of familiar words are some of the most important and useful collocations from a pedagogical point of view. George Woolard makes the point that it is helpful to ask learners which words **they** are surprised to find used together. Teachers need to keep in mind that they may be surprised at what surprises their learners.

We note in passing that this has one very important classroom implication – asking learners if they 'know' a particular collocation is quite definitely testing, not teaching since the idiomatic nature of many collocations means they cannot be predicted with confidence from knowledge of the individual component words. Teachers who forget this risk frustrating learners by asking questions which the learner can only answer by guessing.

One final potential source of confusion should be mentioned. In corpus linguistics the term 'collocation' tends to be used in a different way from the way it is used in this book. Jean Hudson describes it as follows:

> In corpus linguistics it is more often used in the abstract sense of a general tendency for linguistic items to co-occur (not necessarily in immediate proximity): 'I didn't get that job, by the way. The application was in too late.' The words 'job' and 'application' collocate quite strongly, whether or not they are adjacent.

> Much corpus work to date has in fact focused on reporting collocability and patterning, towards the ultimate goal of establishing the most frequent collocates of specific items, with information about the co-occurrence probabilities of words.

This more abstract definition is used in this book only by Michael Hoey, who is, of course, a corpus linguist.

7.6 Colligation

Although many teachers are just beginning to incorporate the explicit teaching of collocation into their teaching, research is also concerned with the it sounded as if one faith had priority – **the** faith, so the organisers have settled on the ungrammatical name *faith zone*, although when anyone asks for it, they will presumably say *Where is the faith zone?* The ambiguity, and hence the problem, could have been solved by calling it *the zone of faith*, precisely because *of* separates the two nouns so that each is **separately** available for pre-modification without ambiguity.

Although LGSWE rightly points out that noun phrases are made in many ways, and that such noun phrases can be very long, it also endorses the view that different kinds of phrases containing *of* are one of the largest sub-categories of noun phrase. Here are a few of the dozen or so types of phrase they list:

species nouns:	*these kinds of questions*
quantifying collectives:	*a set of books*
comparable to genitives:	*the brutal murder of a child*
nouns with *-ful*:	*a mouthful of food*

They also list well over a hundred short phrases – lexical bundles – which contain *of*, and which are typical of academic writing. This small selection gives a flavour of how central such phrases are to this kind of writing:

as a result of	*as a function of*	*from the point of view of*
in the case of	*in terms of*	*in the formation of*
in the direction of	*in the case of a*	*in a number of ways*
in the context of the	*similar to that of*	*with the exception of*
at the time of the	*at the level of*	*at the time of writing*

It is worth noting that this language is precisely the kind of language referred to earlier which is likely to be invisible to learners, whose attention is much more likely to be focussed on difficult content words. If they are to write well, they need to add both kinds of lexical item to their mental lexicons. This will probably not happen without proactive intervention by the teacher.

7.10 Grammar

Sinclair has argued that once we have sufficient corpus-based evidence we may see that our earlier understanding of the role of grammar may have to be revised. He suggests: *Grammar is part of the management of text rather than the focus of meaning-creation.* This description emphasises again that language is first about meaning, and meaning is primarily conveyed by the lexis – words, collocations and fixed expressions – in a text; grammar, although important, plays a subordinate role. This key insight underlies much of this book.

Although there is considerable disagreement about what categories are most appropriate for different purposes, the consensus of opinion among applied linguists is that the separation of grammar and vocabulary as distinct categories is simply wrong. As long ago as 1990, Sinclair claimed:

The evidence becoming available casts grave doubts on the wisdom of postulating separate domains of lexis and syntax.

In similar vein, the authors of the monumental LGSWE observe in their introduction:

Syntax and lexicon are often treated as independent components of English. Analysis of real texts shows, however, that most syntactic structures tend to have an associated set of words or phrases that are frequently used with them.

There is general agreement that there is a spectrum between what is particular and what is general; single words, strong collocations, certain idioms and fixed expressions are invariant, or at least almost invariant, while open collocations, colligations and traditional grammar structures represent varying degrees of generalisability. In other words, we do not simply remember every bit of language we have ever met and list it; we also sort it in some way and make generalisations about it. Michael Hoey has commented: *Grammar is the product of the colligations you have noted in the language* and Sinclair claims: *Grammatical generalizations do not rest on a rigid foundation, but are the accumulation of the patterns of hundreds of individual words and phrases.* Implicit in these comments is the importance of learners meeting large amounts of input which they can use as the basis for their own generalisations. Equally, of course, this view denies that when learners produce correct sentences these are based on abstract 'rules' the learner has been taught; the rules are neither more nor less than various provisional and partial generalisations, based on understanding and breaking down in different ways and to different degrees, input which is essentially lexical.

Grammar often over-generalises

Different 'levels' of language generalise to different degrees. We have seen that words do not occur with other words at random, some words regularly co-occur with other words – lexical collocations such as *strongly suggest, prove conclusively.* Sometimes grammatical features such as articles or prepositions may be part of a pattern – grammatical collocations such as *take the opportunity to.* Colligations are even more general – they relate word to pattern, or pattern to pattern: *I'll see you (time expression); There's no need to (ask/warn/tell/remind etc) (John/your mother/me/ etc).* Grammar structures generalise further, but here a word of warning is necessary. We have already met the idea of blocked collocations; although such collocations are grammatically well-formed and **could** be sanctioned by the native-speaker community, they are not. A source of frustration to learners and teachers alike, they are arbitrarily deemed 'wrong': *We don't say that.* At least this is familiar to teachers, but there has been a tendency to believe that the generalisations of grammar really are true generalisations; Chomsky claimed that a grammar should produce 'all and only' the correct sentences of a language. We now and lead them towards greater autonomy in identifying multi-word chunks in language they are exposed to, and making these more and more part of their communicative repertoire.

Teaching collocation does not mean a radical upheaval, but it does mean a radical change of mindset for the teacher, which produces many small changes in the activities they focus on in the classroom. Learners do become better at noticing, storing and using lexical chunks. We must hope that in due course syllabuses and textbooks will change and the constraints mentioned by Maggie Baigent will become less. Lexis – the merging of grammar and vocabulary, or better still, a refusal to separate them – has more to offer learners than any syllabus based on a limited list of structures and lists of single words.

7.14 Summary

We may summarise the position: given that we now have much better descriptions of English than we have ever had before, and that this reveals that many of the 'rules' previously taught are either wholly or partially inaccurate, things in the classroom must change – no change is not an option. This is precisely the position proposed some years ago in *The Lexical Approach*, but in a recent article Scott Thornbury (*Modern English Teacher,* Vol. 7, No. 4) complains that *The Lexical Approach* does not have a coherent learning theory. In many ways, this is true and the implications are taken up in the next chapter, but a lexical view of language does point to a number of deficiencies in conventional syllabuses. As Karl Popper has so conclusively shown, there is fundamental asymmetry between proof and disproof; we can never, even in principle, prove general statements to be true, but we can, often with comparative ease, demonstrate their untruth. Change and progress are based on disproving the currently accepted view, prompting new theories and experiments, which will provide further evidence and new theories, which in their turn will be disproved.

It is not by any means clear how best to incorporate lexical views into books or courses; at the same time, teachers need to be willing to engage in mini-action research programmes, which they evaluate, not in the hope of finding the holy grail of a 'comprehensive learning theory', but in the hope of providing learners with a more effective learning experience than they had before. The improvement may be substantial or it may be modest, but no change is not an option.

This book is specifically about teaching, rather than describing, collocation. We must, then, ask what may or may not make material more or less teachable, and more importantly still, what aids or impedes learning. So far we have looked at the use of new descriptions of English but, like Timmis, we shall suggest that there are considerable implications for classroom methodology. That is the subject of the next chapter.

Discussion Questions

Do you usually teach new words alone, in collocations or in complete contexts? Why do you follow the procedure you do? Do you think a different procedure might be more effective or more efficient?

Which of the following do you regularly draw to learners' attention: new words, traditional (opaque) idioms, fixed expressions, grammar structures, collocations, clusters?

'Description is not pedagogy.' What implications, if any, do you think the phrasal nature of language has for your classroom?

Chapter 8

Learning in the lexical approach

Michael Lewis

This chapter considers what we know about how languages are learned, and in what circumstances learners are most likely to benefit from the language they meet, both in class and outside. It introduces a clear set of terms for discussing learning. It emphasises the importance of one particular skill – noticing – not recognised on many teacher training courses, and shows how the teacher's ability to select and direct learners' attention to particular kinds of examples is crucial. It discusses and expands the ideas of syllabus and level. It emphasises the importance of meeting new language more than once, and, perhaps to the surprise of many teachers, the relative unimportance of controlled practice. Finally, it discusses why our present understanding of learning suggests real changes in methodology are needed, and how collocation is central to these changes.

8.1 Introduction

Over the last ten years or so, the analysis of computer-based corpora has given us better descriptions of English than have ever been available before but, as we noted in the previous chapter, it is not self-evident that these descriptions impinge directly on the language classroom, and if they do, it requires careful thought to determine how best to modify current classroom procedures. Once again, it is helpful to begin by thinking clearly about terminology, particularly the area covered by the broad terms 'knowledge' and 'learning' and 'teaching'. We need to distinguish two kinds of knowledge – **declarative knowledge** and **procedural knowledge**; secondly, rather than the loose term 'learning', we shall follow Stephen Krashen's distinction between **learning** and **acquisition**. We also need to distinguish **input** from **intake**; identify three separate processes involved when learners meet new language – **noticing**, **sorting**, and **describing**. We distinguish three factors – **accuracy**, **fluency** and **complexity** – which contribute to the overall idea of 'level'. We shall also consider the **non-linear** nature of acquisition, and the implications of **feedback** for the acquisition process. Far from unnecessary theory, a clear understanding of these ideas provides an essential framework for teachers who wish to develop their own understanding.

Teachers sometimes dismiss theory on the grounds that they know from experience that something works. Henry Widdowson has issued two potent challenges to this position – firstly, even if something works, how do you know something else would not work better? Secondly, if you do not know **why** something works, you may be unable to replicate the success, or share it with others. So there is a strong case for understanding why some classroom activities seem to be more effective than others. Everything that happens in class should be consistent with what we know about the nature of both language and learning; equally importantly, nothing which happens in class should violate the nature of either. The previous chapter looked at what we now know about language; this chapter looks at what we now know about learning in general, and language learning in particular.

It is comparatively easy to study what teachers do in class and specify what particular activities are intended to achieve. It is, however, difficult to know what use learners, individually or collectively, make of the language they meet in class and almost impossible to evaluate the effect any particular activity has on learners' long-term language acquisition. However much teachers dislike the idea, the relationship between teaching and learning remains mysterious. Some, like Krashen, even question the value of explicit learning. Less controversially, it is clear that no teaching can guarantee acquisition. As Diane Larsen-Freeman has so eloquently expressed it, we constantly need to remind ourselves that teaching does not cause learning.

We also need to remind ourselves that teaching is never an end in itself; its sole purpose is to facilitate acquisition. Is traditional language teaching likely to achieve this end? If not, what teaching strategies are likely to be more successful?

Teacher training courses often examine what the teacher does, but if we want to understand what is **most** effective in the language classroom, it is with learning, not teaching, that our analysis should begin.

8.2 Two kinds of knowledge

We look first at knowledge in its widest sense. Two different kinds of knowledge have long been recognised – **declarative** and **procedural** knowledge. The first is **knowledge that**, and involves stating facts or rules – the date of the Declaration of Independence, the exchange rate of the pound against the dollar, the past participle of *go*. The second is **knowledge how to**, the ability to actually do something – serve at tennis, drive a car, give a short, witty speech of welcome to a group of visitors.

The two kinds of knowledge are different in important ways. With declarative knowledge, you either know it or you don't; you can remember it (correctly or incorrectly) or forget it; you need to look it up or be told it, directly or indirectly, by someone else; there is nothing to understand, it is simple information, each item separate from each other item. Importantly, the lack of a single piece of such knowledge may be frustrating, or make you look slightly silly, but it will not render you unable to do what you want – if you say *Ever since the Declaration of Independence, whenever that was, seventeen whatever, America has . . .* ; or *I think the company has goed on the wrong line this year . . .* , your message may be badly expressed, but you still, in a more global sense, achieve your purpose.

Procedural knowledge is about global ability; each bit of learning is not **added** to what you already 'knew', but is **integrated into your earlier knowledge**, modifying it in some way. Procedural knowledge is not simple discrete items, but, as its name suggests, sets of complex procedures. New procedural knowledge, once properly acquired, is not 'forgotten' in the way we can forget a date or a new word. Lack of procedural knowledge is likely to leave you unable to **do** something; if you cannot ride a bike, no amount of declarative knowledge about how to ride a bike will help. You cannot look up such knowledge, and no one else can tell you or explain it to you in a way which ensures you will 'know' it. Watching someone else ride may help; but in the end, you have no alternative but to get on, try, fall off, try again and, slowly, you will acquire an **integrated** set of skills which are to do with balance, speed and so on. Once you have acquired the ability to ride, you cannot forget it – it is yours, part of you.

The two kinds of knowledge are not totally separated, but the ways in which we acquire them are. In the examples earlier, the date of the Declaration of Independence is declarative knowledge, **why** America declared independence at that time is complex procedural knowledge; **learning** why in High School is declarative; **understanding** why and relating that understanding to a wide knowledge of American history and politics is procedural. Similarly, the exchange rate on any day is a matter of fact; understanding the movements of the currency market is procedural; the past participle of *go* is a simple fact, but understanding how it is used fluently and accurately is procedural. Stating a grammar rule is declarative knowledge; the ability to use it is procedural. As this last example makes clear, you can 'know' the rule but be unable to use it or you may have mastered the point without being able to state the rule.

> **TASK**
>
> Can you give three examples of procedural knowledge you have and explain how you acquired the knowledge?
>
> How does this knowledge differ from the ways you learned declarative knowledge?

Declarative knowledge is additive, while procedural knowledge is integrative. With a traditional view of language, it is a short step to assume that vocabulary learning – new words – is additive and mastering the grammatical system is essentially integrative, as each bit of 'new' grammar you learn modifies your present intergrammar. A lexical view of language changes the position radically, by abolishing the vocabulary/grammar dichotomy completely. Every lexical item, including single words, has its own individual grammar. This means we can now recognise that **all** language acquisition is

intrinsically procedural. Any discrete bit of language which is learned purely additively cannot contribute to, indeed is not part of, the learner's mental lexicon; although in some sense 'known', it is not available for use. This immediately brings to mind Stephen Krashen's distinction between learning and acquisition.

Learning and acquisition

In *The Natural Approach* Krashen introduced the distinction between language **learning**, which is conscious, and language **acquisition,** which is unconscious. He has controversially claimed that **only** language which is unconsciously acquired is later available for spontaneous use. He claims acquisition is essential, and learning has no value, as what is learned does not contribute to what is acquired. We shall examine this view in some detail, but for the rest of this chapter the term 'learning' is used only in the sense of what is consciously learned; similarly the term 'acquired' is confined to language to which the learner has immediate access for purposes of comprehension or productive use.

If Krashen is right, formal teaching, which is explicitly directed at conscious learning, is effort wasted. Even if he is wrong, and formal presentation and practice of specific items does aid acquisition, our new awareness of the sheer size of the mental lexicon raises immense problems. Any suggestion that teachers could formally 'teach' a lexicon which runs to many tens of thousands (or, for competent native speakers, many hundreds of thousands) of items is clearly unrealistic. If each of 20,000 items took 2 minutes to teach, that is already over 600 classroom hours, more than the total duration of many learners' entire formal language instruction.

This new understanding of the size of the learners' lexical task implies radical changes to the teacher's role. Either teachers must select and teach a restricted lexicon – but on what criteria, for students of general English? – or they must adapt classroom activities so that, rather than teaching individual items, they **provide learners with strategies** which ensure the learners get the maximum benefit from all the language they meet in and, more importantly, outside the formal teaching situation.

8.3 Acquisition and noticing

The basic position of all the contributors to this book partly agrees with Krashen's position, and partly modifies it (in a way he would not accept). Acquisition is accepted as of central importance, but it is suggested that the conscious **noticing** of features of the language that learners meet **does** facilitate acquisition. These ideas need to be explored in more detail.

Acquisition and input

Krashen's claim that we acquire language in one and only one way, by understanding messages, provides a clear starting point from which to examine our presuppositions about how learners do learn – in the loose sense – language. His position is that a learner's interlanguage (the learner's total mental representation of the target language at any moment) is modified by meeting new language which lies on the edge of what the learner already 'knows' in such a way that it is incorporated into the learner's interlanguage so that it is available for spontaneous use.

Not very long ago language teaching emphasised grammar structures and to a lesser extent vocabulary ('new words'). The fundamental assumption was that you first needed structures and, having mastered some central structures, you would move from accurate but halting production, to more fluent speech and writing.

Communicative approaches rightly turned this system on its head. The fundamental emphasis of communicative approaches was and remains that language is about the expression and communication of meaning. This emphasis on 'communicating' inevitably values fluency above accuracy, so the order of priorities is reversed. While this is unquestionably a step in the right direction, it has one unintended side-effect, unless the teacher is exceptionally careful – it places great emphasis on the language that learners produce, so it has a tendency to encourage production, particularly speech, at all times, even in the earliest stages of a course. At the risk of being badly misunderstood, I must point out that you cannot acquire a language by producing it.

Acquisition involves taking in **new** material and incorporating it into the knowledge or skills you already have. Producing language – speech – may make you more confident or may make your speech more automatic or routinised, but that is not the same as expanding your language resources; that involves integrating new language into your intergrammar and mental lexicon.

From input to intake

In addition to introducing the learning/acquisition distinction, Krashen has further claimed that there is only one way in which learners acquire language: *The central hypothesis of the theory is that language acquisition occurs in only one way: by understanding messages. (The Natural Approach).* While there may be much truth in this, it is also true that if you wish to turn the language learners meet – **input** – into language they acquire and have access to for spontaneous use – **intake** – they almost certainly need to notice the linguistic wrapping in which the message is delivered. Exactly what this 'noticing' might involve, and what may help or hinder input becoming intake, is perhaps the most important of all methodological questions.

TASK

Every teacher knows that some of what you teach seems to be acquired very easily by learners but some things that you teach again and again still cause problems for learners.

What factors do you think influence whether input becomes intake?

Do you think it depends mostly on the input language or mostly on the learner's current knowledge?

How important do you think factors such as motivation, tiredness, age or the temperature of the room play?

In this chapter we are mostly concerned with the kind of language input which is needed. It is important to realise that the input which is used in the comprehension of the message may differ from the input which is the raw material for the acquisition of language. Many applied linguists and most teachers believe that, at least to some extent, focussing learners' attention **explicitly on some aspect of the linguistic form** of the input is helpful in accelerating the acquisition process. We need to examine this belief in detail.

You probably make a daily journey from your home to your place of work; the route is completely familiar, and you could give someone else directions for the journey. But do you know the **names** of all the streets you drive or walk down? In all probability you know the route, but you have simply not noticed the names of some of the streets – they are irrelevant when you can achieve your global purpose without attending to such details. The global purpose of language is the communicating of messages; but the medium for doing it is language items – words and phrases – which may need to be noticed if they are to be acquired.

In normal language use, we are usually so predisposed to focus on the message, that the language in which it is delivered is frequently ignored, or, if presented in writing, transparent to the point of being invisible.

TASK

What sort of language which would be useful from an acquisitional point of view do you think your students might fail to notice unless you provided guidance?

Experiments have shown that even quite advanced and motivated learners often do not see the difference between their own effective but inaccurate or unnatural language and a similar correct, natural version which expresses exactly the same content. If they do not notice – see or hear – the differences between the language they used to express something and the correct natural version expressing the same content, then that input **cannot** contribute to intake. Activities which encourage learners to notice certain features of the input probably contribute to the value of the input **specifically from the language acquisition point of view**.

It is essential to remember, however, that the belief that deliberate noticing helps is by no means an established certainty; the current mainstream position is that it probably has at least a facilitative, helpful effect. Explicit noticing is probably a necessary, but not sufficient condition to ensure that input becomes intake.

8.4 Noticing

Second Language Acquisition researchers are somewhat divided over precisely what factors influence what part of input becomes intake. There is a broad consensus that language that is not noticed does not become intake, but there is no agreement on the precise meaning of the word 'noticed'. Even in the most traditional grammar-orientated classrooms, learners acquire vocabulary which must result from accidental, or at least incidental, noticing. For example, while ostensibly studying a structure, learners acquire some of the vocabulary used to exemplify and practise the grammar. Equally, teachers are only too aware that formally teaching a number of words, or requiring students to 'learn these words for homework' is not sufficient to ensure that such items will be committed even to short-term, much less long-term, memory.

Noticing is not quite the straightforward matter it might seem on first meeting the term. In everyday use, the word can refer to both accidental awareness and also to the results of deliberate focussing of attention. It is also the case that sometimes we are able to recall what we accidentally noticed, while on other occasions we cannot recall something to which we paid deliberate attention. Awareness of the potentially wide meaning of the word, should make us very wary about attaching too much importance to any particular kind of noticing in the language class. As always, caution and an open-minded willingness to experiment, and revise our views on effective methodology, is essential.

Given the present stage of our knowledge of acquisition, it is likely to be helpful to make learners explicitly aware of the lexical nature of language (without using that terminology). This means helping learners develop an understanding of the kinds of chunks found in the texts they meet, and the kinds of prefabricated groups of words which are the prerequisite of fluency. This is one part of the teacher's task in encouraging learners not to break the language they meet down too far.

Discussing the value of instruction, of which noticing is a part, Diane Larsen-Freeman comments:

> [several researchers] have pointed out that explicit grammar instruction will not likely result in immediate mastery of specific grammatical items, but suggest nevertheless that explicit instruction does have a value, namely, facilitating input.

Although her comments relate specifically to 'grammar' instruction, they surely apply equally to instruction which ensures learners notice **any** kind of patterning in the input they meet.

Sorting and describing

A word of caution, however. There is a world of difference between the teacher asking *Did you notice . . . ?*, and asking *What did you notice?* Being able to **describe** – verbalise – what you noticed is completely different from actually noticing, or even from being able to sort things according to some more-or-less explicit criterion. Is your new scarf the same colour as your new coat? Have you noticed the difference between the two shades? Can you explain it in words? Would there be any value in being able to do so? Can you describe clearly the difference between two wines you really like? Endless classroom hours have been wasted verbalising grammatical patterns, that is, giving the (supposed) rules. It would be a tragedy if further time was wasted verbalising complex descriptions of lexical patterns, especially when there is no evidence that such descriptions would help acquisition. It could well be that concentrating on such descriptions is an activity which may appeal to teachers, but which is of no benefit to, and indeed may intimidate and confuse, learners. Noticing language helps; **sorting** it into categories or patterns **may** help (see below); **describing** the categories almost certainly does **not**.

Directing learners' attention

Despite any doubts about precisely how noticing helps, it is safe to say that learners frequently do not notice the precise way an idea is expressed, sometimes even if their attention is drawn to it. Some training in the sorts of chunks which make up the texts they read or hear increases the chance of them noticing useful language, rather than many other features which are irrelevant from an acquisition point of view. In *A Cognitive Approach to Language Learning*, Peter Skehan observes:

> Input contains many alternative features for processing, and the learner's task is to extract relevant features which can then be focussed on fruitfully. ...Instruction can work ...by making salient less obvious aspects of the input, so that it is the learner that does the extracting and focussing, but as a function of how he or she has been prepared.

Reporting a major study of noticing by Richard Schmidt, Skehan continues:

> The consequence of Schmidt receiving instruction was that what had been unstructured, undifferentiated input (but whose non-understanding had not impeded understanding very much) became noticeable and analysable, leading to future progress.

In his article (*The Role of Consciousness in Second Language Learning*, Applied Linguistics Vol. 11 No.2) Schmidt points out the crucial difference between information that is perceived and information that is noticed:

> When reading, for example, we are normally aware of (notice) the content of what we are reading, rather than the syntactic peculiarities of the writer's style, the style of type in which the text is set, music playing on the radio in the next room. ...However, we still perceive these competing stimuli and may pay attention to them if we choose.

After a long discussion of the role of consciousness he concludes (the bold is mine):

> I have claimed that subliminal language learning is impossible and that **intake is what learners consciously notice**. This requirement of noticing is meant to apply equally to all aspects of language (lexicon, phonology, grammatical form, pragmatics), and can be incorporated into many different theories of second language acquisition. ...What learners notice is constrained by a number of factors, but incidental learning is certainly possible when task demands focus attention on relevant features of the input.
>
> ...Incidental learning in another sense, **picking up target language forms from input when they do not carry information crucial to the task, appears unlikely** for adults. **Paying attention to language form is hypothesised to be facilitative in all cases**, and may be necessary for adult acquisition of redundant grammatical features. ...Recent psychological theory suggests that implicit learning is possible, but is best characterized as the **gradual accumulation of associations between frequently co-occurring features**, rather than unconscious induction of an abstract rule system.

In summary, learners will ask about input which they do not understand, but teachers need to be proactive in guiding learners toward the input language which is important **from an acquisitional point of view**; the more aware learners are of the chunks of which any text is made, the more likely that the input they notice will contribute to intake.

8.5 The importance of examples

Noticing examples of language in context is central to the acquisition of language, which raises the difficult question of what we mean by **good** examples.

TASK

You are presumably fairly confident that you can identify a chair when you see one but can you define 'a chair'?

Do you think your definition is precise, so that it includes all chairs and excludes benches, stools and other things you might sit on?

Some chairs seem to be better examples of the category 'chair' than others and you almost certainly found while doing the task that the boundaries between similar categories are always fuzzy. It is worth looking more closely at what we mean by a 'good example'.

Until the mid-20th century, it was generally assumed that categorisation was a problem-free procedure, but it is now recognised as a principal source of confusion and error in many disciplines. Philosophers, notably the later work of Wittgenstein, amply demonstrated why this is so. Previously it was assumed that all the members of a category shared a group of characteristics; these could be listed, and membership of the category or class was thus a matter upon which definite and indisputable decisions could be made. Wittgenstein demonstrated that this was not so by considering the concept of 'a game'.

What is 'a game'?

Most of us happily agree that soccer, patience, solitaire, chess, poker, golf, baseball and Tomb Raider (a computer game) are all games. It is difficult, probably impossible, to make a list of criteria so **all** the games satisfy **all** the criteria; despite this difficulty, we are happy to call all the activities 'games'. The difficulty arises from our initial assumption, that **all** the members of a class must share **all** the defining characteristics of the class. In fact, a class is more like a family; all the members share **some**, perhaps most, of a list of defining characteristics; it may even be the case that they **must** share one or more or the characteristics to count as a member of the class. With 'game', for example, criteria include: you can play it, there are rules, it is played between two individuals or teams, it is played in a special place, there is a score, a result, and a winner. We immediately see that some games, which no one doubts **are** games, do not fulfil one or more of these criteria. The implication is that not all members of a category or class are equal; some are better exemplars of the class than others. In the case of 'game', perhaps surprisingly, the only criteria all games seem to fulfil is purely linguistic, you *play* all of them *according to rules*; the only **necessary** characteristics are collocational!

In general, a class is a collection of items all of which share **enough** of the list of defining characteristics to count as members of the class; but some are better examples than others; some of the characteristics may be essential, some important but not essential and some of relatively marginal importance.

The most important fact we need to note is that membership of a class is not the simple matter earlier analyses supposed it to be. In the early days of the Cobuild project Sinclair wrote:

> grammatical generalizations do not rest on a rigid foundation, but are the accumulation of the patterns of hundreds of individual words and phrases. ...The main simplification that is introduced by conventional grammar is merely the decoupling of lexis and syntax.

Feedback means acquisition is non-linear

The simplest way to get an idea of non-linearity is to think of systems in which **feedback** is an intrinsic part of the phenomenon – objects slow down because of friction; the speed is affected by friction, but the friction is affected by the speed, which is affected by the friction and so on. The behaviour of any system which has in-built feedback is difficult to analyse and predict, but such systems are all around us, and language acquisition is self-evidently a natural process in which feedback plays a central role.

Chaos theory is the modern discipline which studies non-linear phenomena, and it provides some surprises compared with classical science. Among its surprises is one of particular interest to us – although you may be able to predict the macro-behaviour of a system, you may not be able to predict the micro-behaviour of the same system. We can, for example, predict the climate with considerable accuracy, but we cannot predict the weather for next weekend with anything like the same certainty; the big picture is clear, but the smaller, more local picture is much less subject to accurate prediction.

It now appears incontrovertible that acquisition is a non-linear phenomenon – what you acquire is a function of the intergrammar you have already acquired, what you notice in the language you meet, which modifies your intergrammar, which affects what you notice and so on; feedback is intrinsic to the process. Even this description is oversimplified, for we must add factors such as forgetting, misunderstanding, successful guesses which were not based on what the learner had fully acquired, and so on. If acquisition is non-linear, no linear syllabus can be adequate.

Sometimes teaching is conducted on the (covert) assumption that examples such as: *It could have been a lot worse, if it had happened during the night. I don't understand how it could have taken three weeks* are assembled bit-by-bit from a knowledge of bits of grammar such as 'uses of *could*' and 'understanding the present perfect' but this assumption is, at best, very questionable.

A more plausible explanation is that the individual learner meets a number of *could have + past participle* examples and understands, or partially understands examples of that colligation used in context. Slowly, an understanding of the nature of colligation itself begins to develop, and **alongside** this, increasing awareness that it can be broken down. **Simultaneously**, the learner has a developing understanding of other multi-word chunks which involve *could*, and other chunks which contain *have + past participle*. The learner begins subconsciously to analyse some or all of these; over a period, with both increased understanding and backsliding co-existing, the learner acquires the ability to analyse several different chunks, and to syntactisise, so that, in due course, there is a permanent change to the learner's interlanguage. Gradually, language which was part of the formulaic memory-based element of the learner's knowledge is transferred to the analytic, rule-based part, thus becoming available to generate new language based on syntactisisation. At this stage real acquisition has taken place.

This non-linear model, which is almost certainly still an over-simplification, is much more likely to represent acquisition than any linear, or even cyclical progression. It could be summarised as 'everything affects everything else', so it is as far as possible from **any** linear model. This kind of model of gradual but permanent change in complex phenomena is currently discussed in many fields. In the study of language itself, it is now a commonplace that when a language is used, it changes; the phenomenon can be summarised in the phrase *When you play the game, you change the rules.*

As Ian Stewart reminded us, for centuries mathematics solved the wrong equations because it clung on to linear models of phenomena which were, in fact, non-linear. It now seems incontrovertible that acquisition is a non-linear phenomenon, so only a non-linear model of acquisition has any chance of representing it adequately. The implication is that linear teaching can never be congruent with non-linear acquisition, explaining Larsen-Freeman's dictum quoted earlier that teaching does not cause learning. She discusses the relationship of non-linear systems and language acquisition in an extended paper (*Chaos, Complexity, Science and Second Language Acquisition* in Applied Linguistics, Vol. 18, No.2). Her comments largely endorse the above:

> The purpose of this article is to call attention to the similarities among complex non-linear systems occurring in nature and language and language acquisition. While the value of the analogy may be only metaphoric, sometimes 'you don't see something until you have the right metaphor to perceive it.' It is my hope that learning about the dynamics of complex non-linear systems will discourage reductionist explanations in matters of concern to second language acquisition researchers.

> Further, learning linguistic items is not a linear process – learners do not master one item and then move on to another. In fact, the learning curve for a single item is not linear either. The curve is filled with peaks and valleys, progress and backsliding.

As we saw in the previous chapter, traditional grammar 'rules' often represent over-generalisations, similar to the phenomena noted by gestalt psychology.

In order to process information, you will be tempted to 'see' the above diagrams as a circle and a square, but careful observation shows they are both incomplete. In order to process information we have a natural tendency to totalise, and thereby simplify our perceptions. This is highly efficient, but it ignores details and implicitly assumes that the details are unimportant. In an attempt to explain everything with a few big generalisations, grammar rules often encourage us to ignore variations which corpus linguistics increasingly reveals are important features of how the language is actually used. In *Corpus Linguistics*, Doug Biber, reporting the results of a massive corpus-based research programme, observes:

> ... a finding that is common in corpus-based research: that overall generalizations of a language are often misleading, because they average out the important differences among registers. As a result, overall generalizations are often not accurate for any variety, instead describing a kind of language that doesn't actually exist at all.

The kind of over-generalisation familiar in grammar is very reminiscent of the powerful, but ultimately unsatisfactory mathematical simplifications described above by Ian Stewart.

8.7 Which is fundamental – lexis or structure?

Syllabuses were traditionally structural, and later the multi-syllabus was introduced, usually based on grammar, vocabulary and skills, but our current understanding of language and learning suggests we may need to re-evaluate the role of grammar in the syllabus.

Our present understanding of the sheer size of the mental lexicon of a competent user of English is deeply dispiriting from the point of view of the learner (or teacher) of English as a second language. It seems the learner needs not several thousand words, but at least tens of thousands of **combinations** of words and mini-patterns. The task seems overwhelming, the more so when we consider how much language production seems to be based on memory, rather than the ability to generate from a few general rules. Within this framework it is essential to re-evaluate what is both possible, helpful and efficient in the classroom.

It must be immediately apparent that any attempt to formally teach and practise the lexicon item by item is impossible, and any attempt to do this would completely overwhelm learners. Fortunately, this is not what a lexical approach suggests. Traditional grammar teaching, with a strong behaviourist streak, emphasised repeated **practice** as a way of fixing patterns; a lexical approach suggests that it is repeated **meetings** with an item, noticing it in context, which converts that item into intake.

Communicative competence is dependent on two parallel systems, a formulaic exemplar-based one and an analytic one, based on generative generalisations or 'rules'. Scott Thornbury, *(Modern English Teacher,* Vol. 7, No. 4)*,* joining the debate on how best to implement the Lexical Approach, says:

A lexical approach provides a justification for the formulaic, unanalysed treatment of a lot more language than has been the case since the advent of the high-analysis era. ...Clearly, the Lexical Approach is work in progress... more research needs to be undertaken, particularly with regard to the part memory plays in second-language learning, and whether (and under what conditions) memorised language becomes analysed language.

He is correct in asserting both that little is yet known about what turns unanalysed language into analysed language, and that this is an important question. What does seem clear is that any analysis performed by the learner is based on inductive generalisation on the basis of language which is already part of the learner's unanalysed intake, rather than formal descriptions or rules. Earlier in the same article, he criticises the Lexical Approach:

Phrasebook-type learning without the acquisition of syntax is ultimately impoverished. ...Fossilization is likely to occur when the learner becomes dependent on lexicalised language at the expense of engaging the syntactisization processes. ...In short, the Lexical Approach lacks a coherent theory of learning and its theory of language is not fully enough elaborated to allow for ready implementation in terms of syllabus specification.

TASK

Imagine an intermediate learner talking to a native speaker who has no experience of teaching her native language. Now imagine yourself talking to the same learner. How would the language you use be different from that used by the inexperienced native speaker?

Which would be of most benefit to the learner? Why?

If you have been teaching for some time, do you think you have got better at changing your language to make it more useful to learners? If so, how have you changed your language?

Do you think the language you use to learners is very precisely targeted or do you use a rather broad range of structures and vocabulary?

How important is paraphrasing and recycling new words and collocations in helping turn the input you provide into intake?

It is an act of faith to assume that it must be possible to specify a syllabus in linguistic terms; indeed, because of the non-linear nature of acquisition discussed above, I do not believe it is possible to do so in any other than very broad terms – the input needs to be (largely) comprehensible and the learners need to be engaged rather than intimidated by the language they meet. It is, I fear, difficult to be more specific than that, bearing in mind that learners in the same class are all at different levels and that they make differential use of any input. This suggests Krashen is broadly right in suggesting that it is the quantity of roughly-tuned input which is the key to acquisition, and that this is in itself the best we can do in specifying a **linguistic** syllabus.

It is also worth reminding ourselves that most learners of a second language never progress beyond some sort of intermediate level. In other words some of their language is, and always will be, fossilised – a repertoire of useful standard prefabricated items together with other language which may be communicatively effective even if it contains 'grammar mistakes'. The fact that their syntactisation processes have not been fully and successfully engaged, rather than invalidating the Lexical Approach, merely acknowledges the inevitable. A combination of 'islands of reliability' which can be used with confidence [see p 175], and language which is communicatively effective even if defective, is surely better than anything any structure-based approach has been able to offer.

Not only does the lexical nature of language and the non-linear nature of acquisition challenge received views of syllabus, however, it also challenges many widespread ideas about methodology. It is to these that we now turn.

8.8 The lexical challenge to methodology

The challenge to conventional syllabuses is based mainly on the non-linear nature of acquisition, while the challenge to methodology is based mainly on the lexical nature of language.

Accuracy and fluency

Perhaps surprisingly, the lexical nature of language represents a considerable challenge to conventional language teaching. Traditionalists value grammar rules and accuracy, believing more or less explicitly that fluency results from the ability to construct first accurately, then accurately and increasingly fluently. An acceptance and understanding of the enormous number of prefabricated chunks of different kinds, implies fluency is based on an adequately large lexicon, and that grammar 'rules' are acquired by learners by a process of observing similarities and differences in the way different chunks work. This reverses our traditional understanding completely – first you need a sufficiently large number of words and larger chunks; this allows some fluency and some generalisations ('rules'). This situation continues for a very long period, and those relatively few second-language learners who do finally achieve a very high standard – that is, they achieve 'accuracy' – do this late in their learning careers as a result of being able to break down chunks into components, and reassemble this in novel ways. This involves both respecting the generalisations represented by the rules and avoiding over-generalisations – many sentences which are grammatically well-formed are not sanctioned as acceptable by native speakers, so accuracy involves knowledge of what is sanctioned and what 'ought' to be but, in fact, is not. The inevitable conclusion is that **accuracy is based on fluency**, not, as was believed for so long, the other way round.

8.9 What do we mean by 'level'?

Fluency and accuracy have traditionally been seen as the two components within the idea of 'level'. Communicative approaches, which are the unquestioned standard in many places, rightly recognise that accuracy is inevitably late-acquired, so learners are encouraged to communicate effectively, albeit defectively, and then to set about improving their production so that it becomes more accurate.

Recent, more precise analysis of the idea of 'proficiency' suggests, however, the more proficient learner uses language which exhibits **three** rather than two distinct characteristics: accuracy, fluency and **complexity**.

The recognition of complexity gives teachers a framework within which to ask *How can I best help my learners to improve their language?* It is immediately clear that different emphases may be appropriate for different learners.

Firstly, awareness of the phrasal nature of the mental lexicon also modifies the idea of a learner's level. An increased lexicon involves different elements:

• Adding new words.
• Expanding knowledge of the collocational field of words already known (including awareness of blocked collocations).
• Increased awareness that 'a word' may have more than one meaning, or be usable as, for example, both a noun and a verb. This corresponds to awareness that a word may have several different, overlapping or even independent collocational fields.
• Knowledge of more colligational patterns – that is, greater knowledge of the grammar of the word, and a correspondingly greater ability to use it fluently, accurately and in more complex patterns.

Secondly, the ideas of prefabricated language in speech and complex noun phrases in writing are particularly helpful in improving the complexity in quite different ways at different levels.

Improving complexity in speech

Modern computer-based studies of spoken and written language confirm, indeed emphasise, what we have long suspected – that fluent speech consists **largely** of rapidly produced short phrases, rather than formally correct 'sentences'. This is as true of relatively formal, educated speech as of any other variety; it is characteristic of all (unscripted) speech, and in no sense substandard. Many of the phrases are relatively fixed, prefabricated lexical items. Access to a comprehensive mental lexicon of such prefabricated units is the basis of fluency in speech. This means learners must be exposed to an adequate amount of natural spoken language. Fluency needs to be based on spoken input, and it is the quantity and quality of that input, not language which learners themselves produce – which is the basis of an adequate lexicon of essential phrases, providing, as we have already seen, that the language chunking is noticed.

Formulaic chunks have been called 'islands of reliability' by several commentators. Chunks which learners are sure are accurate and convey the central meaning of what they wish to say are immensely reassuring, especially when contrasted with the intimidating prospect of constructing everything you want to say word-by-word, on every occasion. Initially, then, the prospect of the lexicon being much larger than we previously thought, is intimidating for learners and teachers alike. However, if teachers can reassure learners, and encourage them to see the value of larger chunks – (semi-)fixed expressions, sentence heads or frames for the pragmatic element of speech, and collocations for the central information content of both speech and writing – these islands of reliability provide important psychological support both in helping learners express themselves within their present linguistic resources, and, equally importantly, as starting points in expanding their mental lexicons. The activity described on page 91 provides a detailed classroom procedure for building on these islands.

Knowledge of fixed items also means additional brainspace is available, so the learners are more able to process other language, which enables them to communicate more complex messages, or simple messages with greater fluency or accuracy.

Improving complexity in writing

At more advanced levels good writing, in particular the kind required of tertiary level students, is characterised not only by accuracy and fluency, but also by complexity. This is largely dependent on the writer's ability to construct noun phrases which are high in informational content. This, as we saw in the previous chapter, implies the text will contain a relatively high number of nouns, which in turn implies frequent use of the word *of*, the single most powerful tool in constructing noun phrases. This is clearly demonstrated by a few sentences from Brian Magee's *Confessions of a Philosopher*; the passage contains 172 words, including no fewer than 13 uses of the word *of*:

> Near the heart **of** the mystery **of** the world must be something to do with the nature **of** time. Neither the time **of** common-sense realism nor the time **of** Newtonian physics is given to us in experience, nor could it be, since it stretches forward and backward to infinity, and nothing infinite can ever be encompassed in observation or experience, Any such time has to be an *idea*, something thought but never observed or experienced, a construction **of** our minds, whether it be a mathematical

calculation or an imaginative assumption presupposed by the deliverance **of** our senses. The same considerations apply to space: the space **of** common sense, stretching as it does to infinity in all directions, is not a possible object of observation or experience – it too is a projection, a construct **of** some kind, as must also be the three-dimensional Euclidean space **of** Newtonian physics... The time and space **of** our experienced reality are forms **of** our sensibility, and it is in that capacity that they appear as dimensions **of** experience.

Notice that most of the *of*-phrases would be entirely absent from or overlooked in regular EFL classes, including those for English for Academic Purposes. Traditional grammar has concentrated on the verb-phrase to such an extent that the construction of complex noun phrases has been largely ignored.

It must be self-evident that for many more advanced learners, the study of noun phrases and expressions with *of* of the kind discussed in the previous chapter are at least one of the keys to learners writing both more fluently **and** at a greater level of complexity.

Competence

Chomsky introduced the terms 'competence' and 'performance' in discussing how the human mind masters and produces language. Performance was language actually produced by people, and thus subject to empirical investigation. Competence was a rather mysterious ability involving knowledge of the rules of (the grammar of the sentences of) a language. Chomsky claimed all performance was based on competence, an abstraction reminiscent of the 'pure forms' of Greek philosophy, and by definition not directly accessible and not subject to empirical investigation. It is astonishing that he got away with inventing a supposedly scientific distinction, one half of which was, by definition, not a scientific concept. (To be scientific, an idea must be testable, and therefore, at least in principle, falsifiable.)

At the beginning of 'the communicative age', Hyams pointed out that language was not an abstract system to be studied by grammarians, but a symbolic system **used** by real people to achieve real, non-linguistic, purposes. Language was a communicative tool. Both words are important – it is a **tool** in the sense that its purpose lies outside itself, it is a means, not an end; the end is communication. If you can communicate anything you wish to on every occasion and do not in the process also communicate things you do not intend, you may be said to possess communicative competence. This is a feature not of the language, but of people or, in classroom terms, learners. Communicative competence **can** be analysed, specified and form a basis for pedagogical decisions. It replaces Chomsky's rarefied abstraction with a concept which is entirely concrete and practical.

We can now go one step further, and ask *What is the basis of communicative competence?* This is an alternative version of the question *What do we mean by (very) advanced learners* – people who can communicate anything they wish, without communicating things they do not intend. Such learners produce language which is fluent, accurate and stylistically appropriate. This involves the learner having a sufficiently large and sufficient phrasal mental lexicon, where many single choices are multi-word items. Jimmie Hill has called this ability **collocational competence**.

As we have already noted, proficiency in a language involves two systems, one formulaic and the other syntactic, and unless the learner can break down input language (analyse) and re-assemble it in novel combinations (synthesise, or syntactisise, using a knowledge of syntax), the learner's language will remain 'impoverished'. The argument in favour of collocational input is that it is easier to break down groups and learn to reassemble them, than to start from isolated words which then have to be combined. As we have already seen, however, language acquisition is a non-linear process, so any idea that we 'start' with groups, and **then** 'break them down' and **then** 'reassemble' them, is very unlikely to be anything other than a partial description of part of acquisition. In the article on *The Lexical Approach* quoted earlier, Thornbury complains that *Lewis does not have a comprehensive learning theory,* and to some extent the criticism is fair. I suggest, however, that few people do. Stephen Krashen has, but it is rejected by everyone to at least some degree. It is also the case that the greatest damage to human understanding has not been caused by those **without** comprehensive theories, but by those with comprehensive theories which turned out to be wrong. A certain humility is required – we simply do not know precisely how language is acquired, and **no** so-called comprehensive theory is more than speculation. We do, however, have partial theories and evidence that certain things do not work. As Thornbury suggests, we need more research; meanwhile we must avoid turning the limited knowledge we do have into a comprehensive theory prematurely. We must guard even more carefully against turning theory into dogma.

'Acquisition' almost certainly involves a non-linear combination of acquiring new words, acquiring new multi-word items, becoming more proficient at breaking large wholes into significant parts (words into morphemes, phrases into words etc), combined with developing awareness – whether explicit or not is a subject of heated debate – of the 'rules' of permitted re-combinations and the restrictions which exclude certain re-combinations.

8.10 Teaching paradigms

The Present-Practise-Produce (P-P-P) paradigm remains a central part of much teacher training. In *The Lexical Approach* I suggested the alternative Observe-Hypothesise-Experiment paradigm, and many of the suggestions in this book endorse and expand this paradigm.

Present-Practise-Produce is intrinsically incoherent as a learning theory. **Presentation** is done by the teacher; **Practice** by learners, moving from controlled to free practice under the direction and time-constraints imposed by the teacher; **Production** is wholly within the learners' domain. The implicit assumption is that teaching **does** cause learning, a view which we have already seen is mistaken.

Any paradigm should, as a minimum requirement, state what **the learners** are doing at different phases of the process. The non-linear nature of acquisition means that different parts of the process may be occurring before, after, or simultaneously with other parts, with different parts of the process being applied by different learners to different parts of the input at the same time. Within this framework, any adequate paradigm is a simplified idealisation of how any individual learner **may** be dealing with some **part** of the input in any given phase of the lesson. However unnerving that is for teachers, or teacher trainers who urge teachers to plan lessons – hence the attraction of the P-P-P paradigm – that diversity is what is happening at any moment in a language class; any theorising to the contrary simply ignores the nature of either language or acquisition.

With those explicit caveats, it is clear that learners do experience a sequence which may be summarised as **meet-muddle-master**. This is essentially the same as Observe-Hypothesise-Experiment. **Observe**: new language must be met **and noticed**. It is precisely on this point that we differ from Krashen's Natural Approach. **Hypothesise**: means sorting the input on the basis of apparently significant similarities and differences – as we have seen, this can be done **without** necessarily being able to describe the categories or sorting process explicitly. **Experiment**: involves using the language on the basis of the learners' current intergrammar (that is, his or her **current best** hypothesis), thereby stimulating new input at the appropriate level to provide examples which confirm or contradict some part of the learners' current hypothesis. Mastery happens – if ever – when new input serves only to confirm the learners' intergrammar.

Within this paradigm, the importance of noticing the difference between what is communicatively effective, and what is formally 'correct' is clear. Learners who believe their output is completely successful will see no reason to modify any of their current intergrammar. Unnoticed deviancy may confirm rather than modify learners' current intergrammar. In addition, teachers have a valuable role to play in predicting problems and providing the negative evidence necessary for effective hypothesis formation, as we see when we consider how the teacher intervenes to direct learners in ways which they are unlikely to use without help.

Teacher intervention

The fact that text – spoken or written – consists largely of multi-word chunks of different kinds, does not stop teachers asking *Are there any words you don't understand?* This question – at least implicitly directing learners' attention to individual words – is misguided for three reasons:

1. It encourages learners to believe that language consists of structures and words, and that single words have unique meanings (and implicit within that is the idea that word-for-word translation is possible).

2. It treats input as if comprehension is the whole story, although as we have already noted, input for acquisitional purposes may differ from simple message-carrying input.

3. It means learners frequently do not invite teacher intervention when that intervention would be immensely useful.

Considering the first point, nothing done in the language classroom should violate the nature of either language or learning, and this question is, as we saw in the previous chapter, based on an out-dated and misguided understanding of the nature of language. It also implicitly encourages learners to approach both text and 'learning' in an unhelpful way.

The learners' intuitive belief that single words are the units of meaning and the frequently mistaken belief that if there is a single word for something in one language, then there must be a single word for it in another, means that unless noticing chunks is explicitly taught, learners left to their own devices are likely to break the text into single words or into chunks which are smaller than the optimal units needed to convert input into maximally useful intake. If learners break the text down into individual words, which they then store as individual words, they make re-encoding much more difficult than it would have been if they had stored the language in larger chunks from the start.

This is also true in the area of pronunciation; twenty years ago Gillian Brown (*Listening to Spoken English,* p 49) suggested:

> There is a certain amount of evidence that native speakers rely very strongly on the stress pattern of a word in order to identify it. It is suggested that we store words under stress patterns, so if a word of a given stress pattern is pronounced, in processing this word, we bring to bear our knowledge of that part of the vocabulary which bears this pattern.

We are now more likely to speak of phrases than individual words, and of a phrasal mental lexicon, rather than someone's 'vocabulary', but otherwise her comments remain valid and relevant. It is very likely that one important way in which we store and access lexical items is by the 'shape' of their stress patterns. Short phrases which have patterns and can be stored with a 'tune', are thus likely to be more memorable than patternless monosyllables.

This counter-intuitive insight, that larger chunks are more useful and easier to store than small chunks, lies at the heart of every idea or activity discussed in this book.

Moving on to the second point, as every classroom teacher knows, it is difficult to move the lesson forward if learners do not understand, so understanding is important. For language to contribute to acquisition it must be (at least partly) understood. But the purpose of input is for it to become intake, and that in turn, must be available for productive use. The ultimate purpose of input is learner output. From this perspective, it is clear that understanding, though necessary, is not sufficient; in addition to **understanding** the input the learner must **notice** the chunks which carry the meaning. Each chunk is a single choice of meaning; if chunks are not noticed **as chunks**, they cannot be stored in the way which facilitates their availability as output. If input is to become optimal intake, **understanding** and **noticing the chunks** are **both** necessary (though perhaps still not sufficient) conditions.

Which brings us to the third point – teacher intervention. Understanding the lexical nature of language makes it increasingly clear that some aspects of language learning are counter-intuitive: phrases are easier to remember than single words; breaking things into smaller pieces does not necessarily make them simpler, and, as we have just seen, understanding is not enough to ensure that input becomes intake. This means teachers need to be proactive in helping learners develop an increasing understanding of the lexical nature of the language they meet and be more directive over which language is particularly worth special attention. This point was exemplified earlier by Morgan Lewis [p 18].

When a patient visits the doctor, the task of diagnosis is exclusively in the hands of the professional. The patient's role is to describe his or her symptoms honestly and clearly, and to take responsibility for following the doctor's advice by, for example, taking the prescribed medicine at the appropriate times, perhaps even choosing between alternative treatments, but the choice of medicine, the choice of which alternatives are offered to the patient is exclusively the responsibility of the professional. So it should be with the language classroom – by all means adopt a learner-centred approach, encouraging learners to take responsibility for their own learning, and allowing choices, but teachers cannot, or at least should not, abdicate responsibility for the syllabus, for deciding which language is worthy of the learners' attention in a particular piece of input, which should in turn have been chosen as suitable for that class. After teacher-directed language activity, it may be appropriate to ask *Is there anything else you would like to ask about?*, but the question *Are there any words you don't understand?* should be banished for ever from the classrooms of competent teachers.

Negative evidence

Because generalisations may be subject to restrictions, language which learners may think is possible, if not actually 'wrong', may be non-standard

of the same input. It is easy to list factors which demonstrate that, although teachers may decide what to teach, they cannot decide what will be learned, much less what will be acquired. Teachers need to adopt strategies which acknowledge the fact that acquisition is irredeemably non-linear.

3. Although using language may help the learner retain it, this is not necessarily so. Using language is stressful – in speech, it involves the difficulty of articulation, working under time constraints, the possibility of error and many other factors which take up brainspace in ways which may make the brain less able to process language, so that it is moved from short-term to long-term memory. Communicative approaches were intended to focus on meaning, but have often been interpreted in ways which have emphasised production, particularly speaking, from the earliest stages of language learning. This runs directly counter to what we know about first language learning, or the way people learn languages naturally when, for example, moving to a new country. While opportunities to speak are essential, and we do not want a return to the silence of old-fashioned grammar/ translation classes, the primary purpose of speaking in class is to increase the learner's confidence; they do not acquire **new** language by speaking, but by listening and reading, subject to making good use of the input they meet.

Successful production may, indeed probably does, help retention, but input not output is the key to long-term improvement in learners' ability. Successful production does not even guarantee retention, as anyone who has hit a wonderful tee-shot while learning to play golf knows. However good the shot was – perfect production – it does not ensure that you can reproduce the performance ever again. Classroom activities which ensure that learners notice input in ways which convert it, or help to convert it, into intake, are more likely to be valuable in the long-term.

The Present-Practise-Produce (P-P-P) paradigm is unrealistic unless the time frame is weeks or months rather than a single lesson or day. Teachers used to the traditional P-P-P paradigm may feel uneasy with the concentration in this book on awareness raising and noticing activities, and the comparative lack of productive practices, perhaps asking – *So when they've noticed it, what do they do with it then?*

In this book all the contributors accept that helping learners to notice useful language accurately, helping them avoid wasting their time on unhelpful activities, guiding their choice of materials and activities, and maintaining motivation may be the principal contributions the teacher can make to learners' acquisition. This is what is meant by seeing the teacher not as an instructor, but as a learning manager. Teachers who feel unhappy with this view may like to consider the way a sports coach operates – it is precisely by accurate observation of a player's performance and the ability to make the player more aware of his or her performance. Sports, like language, involve procedural knowledge and the ability to 'put it all together' under real-world conditions and time-constraints, so that there is often too little mental processing space left to observe your own performance – hence the need for coaches. Knowing what is important, to that player/learner, and ensuring that the player/learner notices what is most likely to benefit him or her at that particular time is a real and valuable role.

4. As we have already noted, understanding the message is not sufficient to ensure that input becomes intake; learners can fail to notice the chunks of which a text is made. Ensuring that they are familiar with the idea of chunks, and developing their ability to identify the chunks they need to expand their lexicons at that particular point in their learning, will help turn input into intake. It is not, however, necessary to give a formal description of any pattern – it is sufficient that learners notice the words, in the correct chunks.

5. Explicit description of the patterns is not necessary and indeed a great deal of time could be wasted labelling patterns. We can all recognise a huge number of colours and sort them into families without necessarily being able to name the families in any precise way. Sorting into fuzzy-edged categories is both all that is needed, and probably all that is possible. The mental lexicon stores items in patterns; more than the few traditional EFL structures, fewer than a vast number of separate lexical items we know – a large number of comparatively restricted patterns. This is done by noticing similarities – we earlier quoted Michael Hoey's observation that grammar is the product of the colligations you have observed. Sorting, consciously or unconsciously, is essential; the ability to describe the sorting categories is not.

8.13 Summary

In this chapter we have noted several important features of acquisition:

- Meeting and (at least partially) understanding the same new language on several occasions is a necessary but not sufficient condition for acquiring the new language.
- Noticing the language chunks which make up the text is again a necessary but not sufficient condition for turning input into intake.
- Noticing similarities, differences, restrictions and examples arbitrarily blocked by usage all contribute to turning input into intake, but formal description of the categories into which input language may be sorted – descriptive 'rules' – probably does not help the process of acquisition, and may hinder it by intimidating some, perhaps many, learners.
- Acquisition is not based on the application of formal rules which generate correct examples, but on an accumulation of examples about which ever-changing provisional generalisations may be made by the individual learner. These generalisations may be the basis for the production of language which is novel for that learner, but all such production is ultimately the product of previously-met examples, not formal rules.
- No linear syllabus can adequately reflect the non-linear nature of acquisition.

These factors, together with the lexical description of language already discussed, give a clear indication of the teacher's role – it is to constantly facilitate the accurate observation by learners of appropriate parts of the input they meet. Put simply, teaching should encourage learners to search constantly for many different small patterns, rather than repeatedly practising the few large patterns of traditional grammar. This serves to remind us that, as we saw in the previous chapter, the Lexical Approach is in important ways more grammatical – that is, pattern-centred – than traditional structural syllabuses.

Discussion Questions

Is there one idea in this chapter which is new for you and with which you strongly agree?

Is there one point about which you strongly disagree?

How often, in your experience, do learners have to meet a new bit of language before you can be fairly sure they will have acquired it?

What role, if any, do you think controlled practices, particularly of grammar points, play in aiding acquisition?

Thinking of your own teaching, to what do you think you will give a) more b) less emphasis as a result of reading this chapter?

Chapter 9

Materials and resources for teaching collocation

Michael Lewis

This chapter explores the importance of choosing texts with the right type of collocational input for particular groups of learners. It also provides a simple introduction to language corpora and concordancing for teachers new to these tools. Although recommending the use of real data, it suggests caution is needed, particularly if learners are to be exposed to raw data. Finally, the chapter comments briefly on dictionaries, particularly collocation dictionaries, as a resource for learners.

9.1 Choosing texts

Collocation is to be found in texts of all types, but different kinds of text have radically different collocational profiles, so two of the teacher's most important skills in the teaching of collocation are choosing the right kinds of text, and then guiding the learners' attention so that they notice those items likely to be of most benefit in expanding those particular learners' lexicons.

In general, fewer words of written English are needed to express the same content than are needed in the spoken mode. This is partly because written English contains many more complex noun phrases and phrases using *of* such as *The choice of texts of different types is conditioned . . . .* Collocations of a small number of key nouns tend to re-occur throughout discursive prose text such as academic writing or a magazine or newspaper article. Newspaper reports (as opposed to articles) contain large numbers of often quite large collocational groups, but many tend to be largely confined to journalism. Although there are motivational advantages to using stories, narratives such as novels or readers are much less collocationally dense, so the use of narrative texts is often an inefficient way of expanding learners' mental lexicons.

Speech, naturally richer in semi-fixed expressions and multi-word adverbials, contains comparatively few of the *verb + (adjective) + noun* combinations which learners need if they are to write essays or reports, and indeed recent research (see particularly the *Longman Grammar of Spoken and Written English* – referred to below as *LGSWE*) suggests major differences not only between speech and writing, but between different genres of speech, or different genres of writing. If learners have immediate specific needs, far from needing a 'balanced' diet of different types of text, the texts to which they are exposed should be skewed in the direction of their needs. For learners of general English, a balance of different text-types is of major importance in building their mental lexicons in a balanced way; no one 'type' of English is remotely adequate to represent the whole. When choosing texts for learner-input, it is important to choose not only from an interest point of view, but also for linguistic, and specifically collocational, reasons.

TASK

Read each of the following texts and:
- Ask what kind of text it is.
- Underline any items which you think are probably stored and produced as multi-word items.
- Now, refine that selection to include only those items suitable for drawing to the attention of a particular class that you know well.

Text 1

Hoverspeed retail director David King said: "With duty rates on alcohol and tobacco continuing to rise in the UK, the market for cross-Channel shopping is growing all the time. Our first store in Scandinavia also demonstrates that we will be looking to expand in other markets where differential tax regimes continue to provide a major incentive for travel retail opportunities."

If duty-free sales are abolished within the EU next year, the firm plans to accelerate its expansion into shops located near ports. Plans for outlets in Ostend, Belgium and Fredrikshavn, Denmark are already well-advanced, and the company expects to expand its retail operation, with additional outlets in Calais and Dieppe.

Text 2

It was a bitter winter. The stormy weather was followed by sleet and snow, and then by a hard frost which did not break till well into February. The animals carried on as best they could with the rebuilding of the windmill, well knowing that the outside world was watching them and that the envious human beings would rejoice and triumph if the mill were not finished on time.

Text 3

The key to understanding the modern analysis of advertising is to understand its functions as a purveyor of messages and information. It is important to distinguish between adverts which provide specific information and those 'image adverts' which present what may be termed non-informational messages. Specific information may relate to price, physical characteristics or other aspects of goods or services mentioned. Such adverts are obviously information-providing. Some adverts, however, such as Marlboro Man, are not generally perceived as providing information except in the broadest sense, but they may still have an important role to play in the marketplace, particularly in relation to the competitive process.

Text 4

After an unsuccessful attempt to win the vice-presidential nomination on the ticket of Adlai Stevenson in 1956, Kennedy began to plan for the presidential election of 1960. He assumed the leadership of the Democratic party's liberal wing and gathered around him a group of talented young political aides, including his brother and campaign manager, Robert F. Kennedy. He won the nomination on the first ballot and campaigned with Senator Lyndon B. Johnson of Texas as his running mate, against Vice-President Richard E. Nixon, the Republican nominee. The issues of defense and economic stagnation were raised in four televised debates in which Kennedy's poised and vigorous performance lent credence to his call for new leadership.

9.2 Genre

If you instantly identified these extracts, it can only be because different types of text – genres – have markedly different linguistic profiles, even if it is difficult to say exactly what makes the profiles different. If learners are to acquire effective and balanced mental lexicons, the range of types of input text to which they are exposed is clearly of great importance.

Text 1, with its mixture of reporting and quotation, use of *job + name – retail director David King* – and explicit detail, is typical of newspaper reporting.

Text 2 is a short paragraph from *Animal Farm*. I am indebted to Chitra Fernando for drawing attention in *Idioms and Idiomaticity* to something George Orwell wrote in 1946 in *Politics and the English Language*:

> This invasion of one's mind by ready-made phrases *(lay the foundations, acquire a radical transformation)* can only be prevented if one is constantly on guard against them, and every such phrase anaesthetises a portion of one's brain.

Considering Orwell's strictures about the use of cliché, it is amusing to note that in as unusual a work as *Animal Farm* he cannot avoid collocations and fixed expressions: *bitter winter, stormy weather, a hard frost, carried on as best they could, the outside world, finished on time*. The point is simply that these items, despite apparently consisting of several words, are in fact single choices in any mature native speaker's mental lexicon – even Orwell's. In short, there is no other convenient way of expressing these concepts, however 'creative' you may wish (or claim) to be. Even the famously creative opening line of *1984*: *It was a bright, cold day in April and the clocks were striking thirteen*, while undoubtedly creative, is based on the collocation *the clock struck*. Collocation is a feature of **all** kinds of text, both spoken and written, though different kinds of text contain different kinds of collocation.

Text 3 is obviously from an information-bearing, text. It includes:
- lexical collocations: *the modern analysis of advertising, the competitive process*

combination of the corpus (a very large one), and the analytical software, produced examples which demonstrably did not meet that criterion. It cannot be said too often that although corpora are invaluable, it is an unjustifiable act of faith to assume that the data they provide is exactly what you need **for a particular group of learners**. If the corpus is one of the large general ones, constructed for lexicographic or descriptive purposes, it may, as Biber observes below, obscure what is of interest to a teacher for a particular class.

Genre-specific corpora

Biber, Conrad and Reppen, (*Corpus Linguistics*, Cambridge University Press, 1998), emphasise how different genres may exhibit very different patterns in the use of both lexis and grammar. They go so far as to warn that huge general corpora may actually **obscure** important patterns which are features of a particular genre, giving as an example the use of the words *deal/deals*:

> The overall corpus frequencies in this case show that *deal/deals* is about equally common as a noun and a verb. This generalisation merely blurs the opposite patterns of use that occur in academic prose and fiction. This small example illustrates a finding that is common in corpus-based research: that overall generalisations of a language are often misleading, because they average out the important differences among registers. As a result, overall generalisations are often not accurate for any variety, instead describing a kind of language that doesn't actually exist at all.

It is clear that if we wish to use corpora for pedagogic purposes, for example, to select teaching materials suitable for particular groups of students, we are likely to learn much more by using smaller, genre- or subject-specific corpora.

Teachers have known this for years; often they would read their Sunday paper – a large corpus – and take an article from it – a small, carefully selected corpus – for use in class. A text is a disguised concordance of certain words, so the teacher who chooses a text for a particular class is simply recognising that a small, appropriately chosen corpus provides excellent concordancing and collocational input for a particular group of learners. This emphasises once again that the single most essential thing about developing or using a corpus is that it must be **designed for a particular purpose**.

Corpora for specific purposes

So, does 'academic English' exist as a definable genre for pedagogical purposes? Do chemistry students need the same language input as the students of fine art, or would two different sets of material be much more appropriate? There are obvious differences in some of the specific vocabulary each group needs, but it is often assumed that they share a need for certain patterns of writing (and to a lesser extent speech) considered typical of so-called 'academic English'. Is this true?

Think of the subject matter – chemists regularly describe processes **under** the control of the experimenter, while students of fine art tend to describe long-term historical processes **outside** the control of any individual; a superficial functional similarity – describing processes – masks a significant difference of lexical and grammatical content. Such differences are reflected in the language which is typical of the particular discipline, so the differences from subject to subject are much more important than previously recognised.

This question can now be investigated empirically. All that is needed is a comparatively small computer-based corpus of the kind of texts the chemistry students will need to understand or produce during their course, and a similar corpus for the fine arts students. Both corpora can be **balanced to take account of what the students will need to do** – read academic texts, attend lectures in their special subject, write an extended dissertation or whatever. A concordancing program will then reveal in a matter of minutes, the **words** the learners most need and the **patterns** in which those words typically occur **in texts related to the particular subject**. It will also reveal whether the needs of the two groups of students can be best met using general 'academic English' materials or whether the groups would benefit considerably more from materials particular to their own field of study.

Biber and his colleagues report just such a study, comparing research articles in ecology and history. They introduce the results by commenting:

> To this point, the analyses in this book have made use of existing corpora to analyze general register categories, such as conversation and academic prose. For studies in ESP, however, a broad sample of texts from academic prose is too general.

Their analysis shows that both academic article-types differ considerably from general fiction, and both share certain features compared with fiction, but it also reveals many important linguistic differences, for example: history articles are more narrative than ecology articles. This means history texts use more past tenses and ecology articles more present simples (for stating generalisations). Ecology articles use more impersonal style, but **certain parts** of history articles also use impersonal style. Their analysis reveals many more details, but in summary it shows that good ESP courses **do** need to be subject-specific, and that 'academic English' is indeed a language teachers' fiction.

It would be professionally incompetent to offer students studying English for specific or academic purposes a diet of general English. It is equally incompetent (though, sadly, it remains not uncommon) to offer them material from magazines devoted to 'popular' science, archaeology or whatever. A decade or more ago John Sinclair stated unequivocally: *At present, selections [of ESP texts] are made on an intuitive basis, and there is no guarantee that a fragment of a text is representative of the book or paper it came from. Quite often, what appears to be introductory matter is offered as typical technical text.* He was criticising the use of introductory rather than body text, precisely because the two are linguistically so different. It is seriously worrying to find that, a decade later, popular journalism on academic subjects – which is even more different from real academic writing than the introductory part of an academic article – is being offered to students of a discipline as suitable preparation for their studies of authentic discipline-specific texts.

Professor Steve Jones who is both a highly esteemed scientist and a regular contributor of scientific articles to the Daily Telegraph newspaper, advises competitors (*Daily Telegraph*, Dec 8 1999) in the paper's competition for young writers on science:

> The rules of science writing differ utterly from those of writing about science. To a scientist, all that matters is to convince an audience trained to pick holes in his argument. Every sentence must be weighed not for style, but for accuracy, every "if" matched with a "but". Terseness is all and elegance much frowned on. ...Writing **about** science demands skills that most of the subject's actual practitioners never bother to acquire.

An expert at both science writing and writing about science, he makes clear that the two genres are radically different. Any teachers tempted to use writing about science as input material for science students need to ensure that they use authentic science writing instead. It should now be abundantly clear that the only suitable material for such students is material which **resembles as closely as possible** the kind they will have to understand or produce themselves.

Focus on 'sub-technical' collocation for ESP learners

Mark Powell has pointed out, from extensive experience with learners with specialist backgrounds, that they frequently know the technical vocabulary of their subject in English, but may well not know the sub-technical vocabulary. This means medical students who know *cardio-vascular* and *ankylosing spondylitis* may not know collocational items such as *straighten your arm, ease the pain*. They may also need to be warned of impossible collocates such as **treat the pain*. This sub-technical vocabulary lies between general English and the technical vocabulary of a particular specialism, and is of great importance to ESP learners, as it is precisely this language which they need to communicate about their specialism to non-specialists, such as patients, supplier or customers.

Building a corpus for your learners

The solution to the ESP teachers' problem is nowadays relatively easy. A comparatively small corpus consisting of research articles in the same discipline can be gathered by asking departmental members to supply a recent paper on disk. As little as a dozen articles will probably reveal key words, and some of their most common collocates **in that genre**, and thus provide an excellent basis for expansion. This can be done by the teacher providing other collocates, with the help of a larger, more general, corpus, a collocation dictionary, or conscious scanning of other subject-based material. Later, students can add further examples from their subject-specific reading.

While searching the internet for material on the Lexical Approach, I found a site listing prepositional phrases from a corpus of material on fine art. Again, a brief sample demonstrates how useful a relatively small subject-specific corpus can be in identifying language that students of that subject will need:

IN

in common, in comparison to, in contrast to, in effect, in private, in progress, in search of, in style

ON

attention on, debate on, effect on, emphasis on, eye on, focus on,
impact on, influence on, reliance on, section on, series on,
on display, on exhibition, on show, on loan

Such language will probably not be noticed by learners in their reading unless they have been trained to recognise its importance for their own writing. It is also clear that many of the items would have benefited by being quoted with one or two more words of the original context. It is a good maxim to remember that there are more chunks than you think, and the chunks are often bigger than you first think.

If learners of general English have a particular interest, it is comparatively easy to download a reasonable quantity of text relating to that interest to form a small corpus, and then use the same techniques to provide a core lexicon of words, collocations and expressions relevant to both the particular subject and the particular learner. In time, learners can be trained to do this themselves. Here is a kind of 'vocabulary teaching' which equips learners to expand their individual mental lexicons in a way which is relevant, personal and a skill which can be taken away as a tool for life.

Caution is needed with raw data

A corpus provides incontrovertible evidence of language which has actually been used but such data needs to be interpreted and used with caution, particularly when used for language teaching. If teachers are going to encourage learners to use corpora themselves, training and even more caution are both needed. One principle of enormous importance is that teachers must become so familiar with authentic examples that they can select out unhelpful examples – however interesting or amusing these might be to the teachers themselves – and direct their learners' attention to a **selection of authentic examples chosen with a particular pedagogic purpose in mind**. By all means introduce learners to authentic examples, but select such examples

structure, which enables the message to be followed without much effort.

Can present and support arguments well.

Is unlikely to make more than occasional errors of grammar, vocabulary or punctuation.

Can write with understanding of the style and content appropriate to the task.

Can produce text which is proof-read and laid-out in accordance with the relevant conventions.

When it comes to assessing formally whether a learner has achieved a target level of CAN-do in the language, statements like the ones above have to be broken down into standardised tasks, so that it is possible to generalise from performance on such tasks the extent to which, for example, the learner is 'unlikely to make more than occasional errors of grammar, vocabulary and punctuation'. From a linguistic analysis point of view, rather than that of the 'lay' user, the learner's language proficiency can be characterised by reference to a set of interrelated competences: communicative, lexico-grammatical, socio-cultural, strategic, etc. How 'proficient' the language learner is can be translated into: where does the learner come in a range of defined levels for these competences appropriate to the use of the language for particular purposes?

In the Cambridge Main Suite EFL examinations 'knowledge and control of the language system' are viewed as underpinning the learner's proficiency in the different language skills and are tested explicitly – at the upper levels through a separate *Use of English* or *English in Use* paper – in addition to any implicit testing of knowledge and control of the language system in skills-based papers such as Reading and Writing.

What exactly (or even inexactly) is involved in 'knowledge and control of the language system' at different levels is not simply an interesting psycholinguistic question; it is a crucial one if, as an Examinations Board, you are attempting to make generalisations about the extent or level of a language learner's 'knowledge and control' on the basis of what words that user either recognises or produces in carrying out certain test tasks.

In investigating this whole area of vocabulary testing we are fortunate at UCLES to have access to the Cambridge Learner Corpus (CLC), a joint project with Cambridge University Press (CUP), for internal research purposes. The CLC is a corpus of written material produced by Cambridge EFL candidates of several different nationalities from Europe and Latin America in response to tasks in the Composition or Writing papers in either FCE, CAE or CPE from 1993 onwards. At the time of writing, it consists of over 8 million words with additions planned. The corpus can be subanalysed by level of examination (FCE, CAE, CPE), and also by candidates' first language. Because the CLC currently has more scripts from CPE than either CAE or FCE, and more from FCE than CAE, frequencies quoted in this article have been weighted to facilitate comparison.

Invaluable though the CLC already is – and we expect it to become increasingly more useful in the future – it is important to bear in mind at all times that the data has obvious limitations. Firstly, it is entirely based on what students have **produced**, not what they can **recognise**. Secondly, even as a sample of what students have produced, it is constrained by the fact that the scripts are a response to specific composition tasks, which inevitably have a strong influence on the language of the topic areas.

10.3 Testing vocabulary knowledge

At the lower levels of proficiency, there may be some justification for a simple quantitative approach to defining levels of 'knowledge and control' of the language; that is, you could simply count the number of grammatical constructions and headwords that a learner is expected to be familiar with in terms of recognition or production at a given level. So an elementary level learner might be expected to be familiar with, say, 1300 words such as a good vocabulary book might present and practise, while an intermediate learner might need these 1300, plus perhaps another 1200 or so 'more difficult' (ie less frequent or more complex) words.

The simple quantitative approach may be studied by comparing the frequency of occurrence of headwords across CPE and FCE in the CLC and also with large corpora based on native-speaker use. These comparisons reveal some obvious facts:

• CPE students use significantly more different words than FCE students.
• CPE students use more low frequency words than FCE students where 'low frequency' relates to citations in native-speaker based corpora.

1. Counting headwords

Perhaps more interestingly, however, the conclusions that can be drawn about learners' lexical knowledge at different levels from simple frequency of occurrence of headwords are distinctly limited. A search of the CLC for a number of randomly chosen words which occur at either CPE or FCE level in the CLC and have a low frequency in native-speaker corpora (*designation, unfavourable, snag, circulate, whine, stretcher, earthy, lik(e)able, puny, barmaid, self-supporting, pin-stripe*) reveals the following: three occur at **both** FCE and CPE level (*unfavourable, stretcher* and *lik(e)able*) and seven occur **only** at CPE level (*designation, snag, whine, earthy, puny, self-supporting* and *pin-stripe*) but two occur only at FCE level (*circulate, barmaid*) – which perhaps tells us more about the social habits of FCE students than about their vocabulary level!

Testing familiarity with a number of different headwords can provide us with information about the 'quantity' of headwords in a learner's vocabulary resource, and even some limited information about the learner's knowledge of the grammatical significance of those words. At UCLES we will be using the CLC to develop the quantitative aspect of the characterisation of vocabulary knowledge further as part of the definition of what is typically expected of learners at a given level. We will also continue to include tests in the UCLES Main Suite examinations which are designed to probe how extensive the learner's knowledge is in terms of knowing cumulatively more headwords related to the appropriate language functions.

However, there is clearly much more to the jigsaw of a learner's vocabulary knowledge than simply familiarity with more or fewer headwords.

2. Parts of speech in vocabulary knowledge

Even on the level of simple familiarity with headwords, it is possible to probe whether the learner has acquired some vocabulary knowledge which has grammatical significance. Take, for example, words in the same family such as *deny* and *denial*. In the CLC, the weighted frequencies of *deny* at FCE and CPE levels respectively are 46 and 120; *denial(s)* occurs only at CPE level (with a weighted frequency of 2). From this we might deduce, with the usual caveats about the sampling limitations of the CLC, that both FCE and CPE learners are familiar with what is meant by 'denying' but there is no evidence to date that FCE level learners are able to produce the nominal form *denial*.

The learner's knowledge of what 'part of speech' a word is – whether it has the grammatical property of being a verb (*deny*) or a noun (*denial*), or occurrence as either a noun or a verb depending on the co-text (for example, *claim*) – can in fact be tested directly without, of course, involving any reference to terminology such as noun or verb, as in this example:

> Only one of the following words can occur in **both** blanks in the sentence below. Please circle the appropriate letter:
>
> **A** assert   **B** claim   **C** insist   **D** presume
>
> He had the nerve to . . . . that we all agreed with him, but I totally repudiated that . . . .

If a learner's answer demonstrates that (s)he knows that only *claim* can occur in **both** slots, what does this tell us about her/his vocabulary knowledge? Bearing in mind that we would need to have the evidence of a number of responses to such items before making any generalisation, we can deduce that the learner's knowledge goes beyond simple familiarity with the headword.

Analysis of citations in the FCE and CPE subcorpora in the CLC indicates the following weighted frequencies for verbal (*claim, claims, claimed, claiming*), and nominal forms (*claim, claims*) of the 'word' *claim*:

Weighted CLC	FCE	CPE
Verbal forms of *claim*	38	132
Nominal forms of *claim*	2	18

On the evidence of the large native-speaker based corpora, verbal uses of *claim* appear to be about one and a half times as frequent as nominal uses in the writing of native-speakers. As can be seen from the above table, in the CLC the nominal uses of *claim* are generally much less frequent than the verbal uses when compared to the native-speaker data, but are also much rarer at FCE level than CPE. The evidence suggests that we might expect learners at CPE level, but not FCE level, to be able to use and recognise *claim* **both** as a verb and as a noun.

One of the many caveats that needs to be mentioned here in connection with derivationally related words like *deny* and *denial* is that there can be no assumption of priority of one particular grammatical form of a word over another grammatical form. For example, because the noun form *denial* is found in CPE citations of CLC, one could not automatically deduce that forms of the verb *deny* would necessarily be found or be more frequent – or 'less difficult'– than the noun form *denial*. Looking through the CLC for forms of the verb *insinuate*, and the noun *insinuation*, which I will be referring to later on, I noted that only the form *insinuating* is found in the CLC, and at CPE level. This mirrors the fact that in large native-speaker corpora *insinuating* is more frequent than any of the other verb forms of *insinuate* or of the noun form(s) *insinuation(s)*.

3. Dependent grammar patterns in vocabulary knowledge

The grammar of words clearly extends far beyond the basic level of whether a word occurs as a verb or noun or both; it also involves the word's dependent patterns and constructions, and this is one of the most significant areas in differentiating a learner's knowledge of vocabulary at various levels. At the risk of stating the obvious, I am distinguishing here, on the one hand, the knowledge of a grammatical pattern or construction (eg how to form a *that*-clause) from, on the other hand, the knowledge that a particular vocabulary item **occurs** with that pattern or construction (eg that *claim* occurs with a *that*-clause). The latter is what I mean when I refer to knowledge of the grammar of words.

We already know that familiarity with *claim* as a noun but not as a verb is a likely distinguishing feature between FCE and CPE learners in the area of production at least. We might now wish to probe whether there are grammatical patterns which occur with *claim* as a verb which might provide more subtle distinguishing features of the knowledge of the word *claim*. CLC evidence indicates that 26 of the 38 weighted occurrences of the FCE citations of *claim* as a verb have a following *that*-clause, *(They claim that road conditions aren't safe)* but only 2 have a following *to*-infinitive construction

(She claimed to have a fish bone in her throat). These figures contrast with 68 occurrences of *claim* + *that*-clause and 17 of *claim* + *to*-infinitive in the CPE citations.

Knowledge of these two grammatical patterns of *claim* could be tested in items such as the following:

> Only one of the following words can occur in **both** of the blanks in the two sentences below. Please circle the appropriate letter:
>
> **A** believes   **B** tends   **C** boasts   **D** claims
>
> She . . . . that she is more accurate than her sister in her work.
> She . . . . to be more accurate than her sister in her work.

Similarly, words with more complex patterning, such as the three patterns for *remember*, which all occur at CPE level in CLC, could be tested with items such as:

> Only one of the words in A, B, C, D is appropriate in **all three** of the blanks in the three sentences below. Please circle the appropriate letter:
>
> **A** remember   **B** agree   **C** suggest   **D** admit
>
> She did not . . . . posting the letter.
> She did not . . . . to post the letter.
> She did not . . . . that she had posted the letter.

The difference between multiple co-text test items such as those in the example above and traditional test items based on choosing a word to fit a single sentence, is that the implicit assumption that knowledge of a word is cumulative as the learner reaches a higher level is made explicit. This is done by requiring the learner to demonstrate greater knowledge of a word's properties and patterns, signalled by selecting or producing a word which is acceptable in a range of different co-texts.

This is not to underestimate the fact that testing patterns in depth in this way is not entirely straightforward. Take, for example, the question of level. Test items constructed for a particular level of examination need to discriminate between learners **clustered around that level** with a view to classifying them as having adequate, good, exceptional, etc ability **in relation to that level**. Such tests are **not** designed to discriminate across **widely separated levels of proficiency**. Hence, since *claim* followed by a *that* clause is a feature of *claim* which is expected to be known at FCE level, it is probably redundant to include this pattern as a CPE level test item. For a CPE level test, a vocabulary item which occurs in CLC only at CPE and CAE levels and not at all at FCE is likely to discriminate better. For example, knowledge of the grammatical patterns of the verb *dread*, which is found in CLC at CPE and CAE levels with both *to*-infinitive (*Old people dread to go*) and with verb + *ing* (*I even dread thinking about the winter*), might be tested instead of *claim*:

Only one of the following words can occur in **both** of the blanks in the two sentences below. Please circle the appropriate letter:

A avoid   **B** refuse   **C** dread   **D** hesitate

I . . . . to contemplate the future.
I . . . . contemplating the future.

The beneficial effect on vocabulary learning of such items is the way in which they illustrate the layers of grammatical patterns which make up knowledge of the grammar of words. An equally important teaching point that should be made is that it is comparatively rare for apparently parallel constructions to be freely interchangeable without some change in meaning or some restriction on use. An obvious example, repeated from above, is the difference between *She did not remember to post the letter, She did not remember posting the letter*, and *She did not remember that she had posted the letter*, where the first entails that she did **not** post the letter, in the second it is an open question whether she posted the letter or not, and the third entails that she **did** post the letter.

There are also more subtle differences associated with grammatical properties, to which I shall return when discussing collocation below. For example, when *dread* is followed by *to*-infinitive the verb in the infinitive is usually in the semantic field of imagination such as *contemplate, see, think* and **under** the control of the subject of *dread*. For something **out of** the control of the subject such as *fall ill*, the verb + *ing* construction with *dread* seems much more natural. For example:

? I dread to fall ill while I am travelling.
I dread falling ill while I am travelling.

There are practical problems associated with such test items with regard to sustainability, by which I mean the difficulty of constructing such items over a sustained period, so as to ensure consistent and adequate sampling of the learner's knowledge of the grammatical properties of words, and not just testing what is relatively easy to test.

4. Collocations and vocabulary knowledge

So far I have dealt with three important pieces in the jigsaw of the learner's lexicon – simple familiarity with a quantity of headwords used in connection with the functions and topics appropriate to a particular level of language proficiency, and two aspects of familiarity with the grammatical properties of words: their word category and dependent patterns and constructions. That still leaves a lot of uncharted or unpredictable territory in the jigsaw, and this is where collocation enters the frame.

The term 'collocation' has been well established in the description of language since the days of Firth. It is usually contrasted with 'colligation' as in the definition in Robins (1964:234):

Combination with *claim*	Category
luggage, baggage	Free collocations
compensation, benefit, allowance	Restricted collocations level 1
attention, credit	Restricted collocations level 2
lives	Restricted collocations level 3
stake (stake *a* claim)	Figurative idiom
lay (lay claim to – not *lay *a/the* claim to)	Pure idiom

No doubt there may be other equally arguable positions as to precisely which level of restricted collocation is appropriate for some of the combinations in the table above. My concern is mainly to illustrate the principle of the continuum of relationships which combinations of lexical items can enter into.

Howarth suggests that learners' lexical difficulties lie chiefly in the restricted collocations 'since idioms and free collocations are largely unproblematic'. He concludes:

> A comparison between [Native-speaker] performance and [Non-native-speaker] errors suggest that at an advanced level learners are lexically competent and have successfully internalised the more restricted collocations and semi-idioms. There remains, however, the vast hinterland of less restricted combinations . . .

10.5 Sources – native-speaker corpora and dictionaries

One of the most fertile sources for sampling the grammar of words and collocations appropriate to different levels of proficiency, especially the higher levels, are the large native-speaker corpora, part of which are now available in some limited form via the Internet. These provide a range of examples and useful frequency data but they must be used with considerable caution – it is always necessary to bear in mind the differences between the purposes for which corpora were produced, and the students' vocabulary needs in relation to the specific syllabus or learning goals they are following.

My searches of the large native-speaker corpora to date have confirmed that these corpora provide only a partial selection of all the patterns or collocates one would expect to find for a given lexical item – nor do they come with an absolute guarantee that what you do find in them would be accepted as standard English. Searching through the occurrences of *sincerity* to check on any occurrences of *sincerity* as subject noun with *frighten* as in Chomsky's non-deviant sentence above, I was amused to find that there **was** one citation, namely Chomky's own sentence quoted from a book on language as a 'somewhat peculiar example'.

I also found among the dependent patterns of *sincerity* an example of *for*+ verb+*ing* as in *he had no sincerity for finding solutions* – not, I think, a pattern that would be judged to be standard English. And as a diversion, I stumbled on a special kind of millennium bug in the large native-speaker corpora: it appears that about one sixth of the large number of citations of *millennium* are spelled with only one 'n'. Should we take the fact that this spelling with one 'n' occurs in significant numbers of native-speaker citations as sufficient proof that *millenium* is an acceptable alternative spelling?

If occurrence of a dependent pattern or collocation in the large native-speaker corpora does not necessarily guarantee that the pattern or collocation **is** standard English, it is also true that **non**-occurrence of a particular dependent pattern or collocation in the corpora (or occurrence in less than a statistically significant frequency) is by no means a guarantee that such a pattern or collocation is non-standard or unacceptable.

Returning to an earlier example, here is the entry for *insinuation* in the *LTP Dictionary of Selected Collocations* (DOSC):

INSINUATION
V: defend oneself against, deny, make, (dis)prove, reject ~
A: horrible, nasty, serious, unfair ~

Where V: indicates that the cited verbs or verb phrases collocate with *insinuation* as object, and A: indicates that the cited items collocate as adjectives with *insinuation*. Examining large corpora, however, I compiled the following:

V: ooze, resent, wince at ~
A: astronomical, clear, disparaging, filthy, foolish, heinous,
   hidden, indirect, silent

Intuitively, the DOSC list of collocations looks to be a familiar selection of verbs and adjectives that one might expect to come across or use with *insinuation*, but the overlap with the comparable collocations in the corpora happens to be minimal.

Native-speaker corpora are clearly very valuable as sources of authentic learning and testing material, and for checking on frequencies, and typical co-texts of lexical items, such as the fact that *deny*, referred to above, is almost invariably used negatively – *I cannot deny . . .* – or in question form such as *Who would deny . . . ?* UCLES' approach to producing items for testing English in use at various levels, whether with a grammatical or lexical focus, is what is sometimes referred to nowadays as 'corpus-informed', not corpus-based. When it comes to dependent patterns and collocations, the native-speaker corpora need to be used in conjunction with other reference material such as advanced grammars and collocation dictionaries.

10.6 Sources – the learner corpus (CLC)

As I have suggested above, the CLC is already proving invaluable in helping us at UCLES to build up a picture of the vocabulary knowledge associated (albeit in productive medium) with different levels of proficiency (FCE, CAE,

CPE), for example, in terms of number and frequency of headwords at each level and evidence of the range of grammatical patterns used with particular words at each level. It is certain to prove equally valuable as a source of collocations which might be expected to be known by students at different levels, especially when used in conjunction with the native-speaker corpora and well-researched collocation dictionaries.

A particularly interesting and fruitful area of collocations for both teaching and testing purposes, emerging from searches of the CLC, are those collocations which are made up of words which individually have a very different frequency from their frequency as collocations. Take, for example, the word *opinion*. As one might predict, *opinion* is very frequent in the CLC across all three levels FCE, CAE, CPE because composition tasks frequently require the candidate to express opinions. The verb *form* also occurs in CLC at all three levels, least often at FCE (10 weighted occurrences). However, the collocation *form~opinion* occurs only at CPE level (9 occurrences).

Going through all the verbs listed in DOSC with *opinion* as object, the weighted frequencies in CLC are as follows:

	CPE	CAE	FCE
accept	5	2	
agree with	6	2	47
ask (for)	6	6	8
change	10	4	8
confirm		2	
express	10	40	10
form	4		
give	11	34	44
have	70	34	94
impose	1		
influence	1	2	1
offer	1		1
state	1		

There are no entries in the CLC at any level for the following verbs listed in DOSC as collocates of *opinion*: *air, convey, discount, dissent from, endorse, modify, mould, seek out, stick to, sway, trust, venture, voice*.

The verbs from DOSC are not, of course, the only verbs which collocate with *opinion* as object. Here are some other examples from the CLC not in the DOSC entry for *opinion*:

	CPE	CAE	FCE
justify		2	1
object to	1		3
respect	1		2
share	9	9	12
value	2		

From this kind of data we may be able to start building up a picture of incremental ranges of collocations which are significant in characterising lexical knowledge at different levels of proficiency, especially those involving vocabulary items, which, looked at in isolation, have frequency profiles which would not automatically lead us to associate them with different levels of proficiency.

10.7 Approaches to testing collocation

Tests involving recognition of appropriate collocations are a standard part of UCLES' examinations. Some typical examples of collocations from CPE Paper 1 are listed below together with the relevant test item. The test focus part of the collocations is in bold:

1. **breach**~code (of ethics)
   Any doctor who . . . . the medical profession's code of ethics is severely reprimanded.
   A fractures   **B** cracks   **C** ruptures   **D** breaches

2. **pursue**~point
   She obviously didn't want to discuss the matter so I didn't . . . . the point.
   A maintain   **B** follow   **C** pursue   **D** chase

3. lend~**weight** (to)
   These documents lend . . . . to the reporter's accusations.
   A depth   **B** weight   **C** volume   **D** gravity

4. power~**wane**
   This is the author's tenth book and it is clear that her creative power has . . . .
   A waned   **B** dissolved   **C** suspended   **D** dispelled

It should be noted here that in selecting the appropriate collocation, the learner also decides that the so-called distractors, when inserted in the gaps, actually form deviant expressions, such as *to rupture a code of ethics, *to chase a point, *to lend gravity to something. It is worth noting, therefore, that successful performance on such test items involves knowing **both** what is possible **and** what is not.

Testing collocations in this way has worked well enough over the years in that performance on such tests correlates well with other measures of high-level language ability used in the CPE. As part of the process of developing a revised version of CPE (due to be introduced in December 2002), work is being carried out on corpora to check on frequencies, among other criteria, for establishing appropriate difficulty levels of such collocations.

Experimental test formats are also being trialled, which attempt to probe the cumulative nature of lexical knowledge as evidenced by the learner's ability

Lightning Source UK Ltd.
Milton Keynes UK
UKOW04f1811290317

297853UK00001B/2/P